My Time with Ela Gandhi

Susan R. Easterbrooks

Edited by Lynn Skapyak Harlin
Cover design and layout by Richard Levine

The stage photo of Ela Gandhi and Donna Lowry courtesy of Donna Lowry and Georgia State University. All other photos courtesy of Ela Gandhi or by the author.

Published by Hidden Owl, LLC,
hiddenowl.com

ISBN 978-0-9962371-8-5

Printed in the United States of America

For my granddaughter, Audrey. May she grow up to live in a safe and principled world.

Contents

Acknowledgments

I owe a debt of gratitude to a long list of people. First and foremost are Dr. Gwen Benson, Associate Dean, and Dr. Susan "Sue" Ogletree, Director of the Center for Evaluation & Research both of the College of Education and Human Development, Georgia State University, who invited me to go to Durban and who described their experiences as relayed in *The Freedom Ride* chapter. They also read several sections of the work in progress. Thank you, Ladies. My thanks also go to Mr. Tim Merritt, GSU videographer, who provided me with a copy of Ms. Gandhi's talk.

Dr. Laverne Samuels, Director of International Education and Partnerships of Durban University of Technology, shared memories of his interactions with Ela. Thank you, Dr. Samuels.

Satish Dhupelia, Ela's nephew, whose mother is Sita, Ela's sister, sat at his computer for many unrewarded hours to provide additional insights and to verify depictions I created from various sources of information. Thank you, Mr. Dhupelia. Asha and Kidar Ramgobin, two of Ms. Gandhi's children, also advised me on various subjects. Mr. Ramgobin is on the Board of the Gandhi Development Trust.

Expressions of thanks must also go to the kind friends and family who did initial readings of pieces as they were written: Cheryl Easterbrooks, my sister, Dewey Troutman, my husband, Dr. Marc Marschark, founding Editor of the *Journal of Deaf Studies and Deaf Education*, and Dr. Alex Lichtenstein, Professor of History, Indiana University and Editor of the *American Historical Review*.

Several generous souls also read the entire first draft upon its completion and made additional suggestions. These include Helen Litterst, former Director of the Rhode Island School for the Deaf, Pat Gorham of Richmond, VA, Roberta and Randy Perry of Carefree, AZ, and Roberta Ingenito of Gainesville, GA.

The Director of The National Gandhi Museum in New Delhi graciously showed me around the museum during a 2012 visit to

India, allowing me to see with my own eyes the written works of the Great Mahatma. Many thanks to the staff there.

Special thanks go to my husband whom I abandoned for the computer on far too many occasions. Thank you for helping me remember the details of our adventure.

And last but by no means least, I am indebted to my editor, Lynn Skapyak Harlin. I thought I knew how to write, but you opened my eyes to the world beyond academic writing and I am excited about new possibilities. Your direct manner, insistence on accurate style, and constant encouragement are why this book was completed. Thank you from the bottom of my heart.

Before proceeding, the reader might like to listen to Ela's voice and see her demeanor during an interview at Georgia State University. This may help you imagine her voice as you read the words it was my honor to write down.

https://mediaspace.gsu.edu/media/Ela+Gandhi%2C+22nd+Benj amin+E+Mays+Lecture/1_cvkx1b6p

Chapter 1

Crossing the Northeastern to Southwestern Hemispheres

All heads turned to the lone woman walking through the door. The patrons seated at tables looked at her with smiles, their comments to one another hidden behind hands discreetly raised to their mouths. It was obvious most people in the room knew who she was and found pleasure in seeing her. She returned all smiles with a gentle nod of her head and an acknowledging smile of her own.

Diminutive, dressed in a tasteful white Punjabi outfit with a beige shawl over one shoulder, Ela Gandhi (Ela is pronounced with a long e) walked in our direction, all eyes on her. Seventy years old at the time of our first meeting, she was short with neatly combed, graying, nape-length, thick dark hair.

There was an interesting ambience in the room, almost as if it were from a bygone era, British Colonial, with substantial and ornate heavy wooden furniture and lush, dramatic drapery. I had the sense I was in an old-time movie, half-expecting a monocle-sporting British officer toting an elephant gun to appear.

It was April 2010. I had the great good fortune to undertake the unexpected adventure of a lifetime to Durban, a city in the Kwa Zulu Natal Province of South Africa.

The trip to Durban was rather arduous. I had been on many planes before, but never had I been on a 17-hour direct flight. The initial excitement I felt boarding the plane soon wore off. Hour after hour after hour of mind-numbing flight in limb-cramping seats takes a toll on both body and spirit. My enthusiasm returned when we finally arrived in Johannesburg from Atlanta.

Prior to this first trip to KwaZulu Natal, a thought occurred to me. I live near the seat of the Eastern Band of the Cherokee Indians.

Perhaps I could facilitate a conversation between the leaders of the Cherokee and Zulu nations. Both are indigenous cultures. Perhaps they could share information about how they are resolving their mutual struggles.

This was an uncharacteristically bold plan. I'm a bit of a loner. Nevertheless, I cold called the office of Principal Chief Hicks.

"Chief Hicks is not in the office at the moment," the young man on the other end of the phone said. "May I take a message?"

"Yes, thank you," I said. "I am a member of a group traveling to the KwaZulu Natal province in South Africa. I would like to talk with your chief about establishing a contact between your two nations."

"I will discuss this with the chief and call you back," he said.

"Thank you," I said. "I hope to hear from you soon." The line went silent.

Well, that's the last of it. I'm sure they have better things to worry about than my request.

But several days later I received a call from the same young man.

"The chief is able to see you next Thursday at 3:00, if that is suitable with you," he said.

"Absolutely," I said, "And please thank the chief in advance for me. I will be there."

On Thursday, my sister, Cheryl, drove up to North Carolina with me.

"I always forget how lush and green the foothills of the Smoky Mountains are," I said. The trees grew in density the higher we climbed. Periodic pull-outs from the road winding up the mountains allowed for spectacular views.

"Oh shoot," said Cheryl. Her sudden statement caused me to jump.

"What," I said. Then I saw it. The roadway was closed for repairs. Heavy, black tar trucks were spewing their contents onto the ground. The dense chemical scent of tar wafted through the air-conditioner vents.

"Oh please," I said to no one in particular. "Let us go around. We're going to be late." I drummed my fingers uselessly on the steering wheel.

"It doesn't matter," Cheryl said. "We'll get there when we get there."

And I'm on a fool's errand anyway. I don't have any real plans in mind.

"I don't know what I was thinking," I said. "It seemed like a good idea at the time. I don't know what possessed me."

"It's who you are," she said. She took a scarf out of her purse and covered her nose. The stench of the tar was oppressive.

"But I don't want to be late," I said. "That would be embarrassing. Here I am asking for a favor and I show up late."

"Not much you can do about it," she said.

Luckily, the pilot car returned, and we followed it around the chaos, freed to continue our ascent up the mountain. We drove into the town of Cherokee, the seat of the Eastern Band of the Cherokee Indians, an hour late for the appointment.

I'm mortified. I hope he understands.

The town was small, running alongside the Oconaluftee River between the Smokies and the Blue Ridge Mountains. We parked outside the low, biscuit-colored administration building. We followed the signs to the office.

"Hello," said the young man in the office. "I am afraid the chief had to leave."

"I am so sorry," I said. I explained why we were late.

"Please take a seat," said the young man. He placed a call on his phone and left the room. His conversation was muffled by the walls. In a few minutes he reappeared.

"The chief will see you when he returns," he said.

"Oh, thank you so much," I said. "Do you have any idea of how long that will be?"

"No," he said.

He left us. The place went quiet. The heavy kind of quiet you feel half-way up a trail, with all sounds muted by the earth and trees surrounding you. We sat. We looked around the office. We waited.

The building was like any other municipal building in any other small-town southern community. Wooden paneled walls. Well-worn carpet. Pictures of important citizens on the walls. And artifacts of the town's important history, its struggles to regain its stature in the wake of the Indian Removal Act of 1830, signed by Andrew Jackson. This sent 125,000 native Americans from North Carolina, Georgia, Tennessee, and Florida upon the treacherous Trail of Tears.

In about 20 minutes, the young man returned. He was slender, his hair ruffled from the wind outside the building.

"The chief will see you now," he said.

We entered Chief Hicks' office.

My, but he's a handsome young man. Slightly taller than I. Strong. Younger than I imagined he'd be or maybe I'm older than I think I am.

Chief Hicks extended his hand in greeting. He had high cheek-bones and almond-shaped eyes. He wore an orange shirt, the color of the flag of the Cherokee nation.

"Please accept my apologies for being late," I said. "We encountered roadwork on the way up the mountain." He waved his hand, dismissing my concerns.

"How may I help you?" he said. He took a seat in the standard-issue swivel rocker behind his well-polished wooden desk.

I explained my wish to introduce the two leaders to one another. Chief Hicks was gracious and listened to my scheme. He suggested ways in which the two leaders could communicate.

Our conversation ended and he walked over to some shelves with beautiful woven baskets on them.

Chief Hicks and the Author

"Please give this basket to the King with my regards," he said. "It was woven by a member of our community."

Cheryl took our picture with my old Sony camera.

"Thank you," I said. "You have been most gracious."

So nice. So generous with his time even though I was late. I am so lucky to have met him.

We left the office, turned onto the bridge over the river running through town, and headed out of Cherokee for the drive back down the mountain to our home in North Georgia.

That is how I found myself carrying this lovely Cherokee basket through the airport in Johannesburg, South Africa to catch the last flight to the eastern coast of the country. It sat on my lap in the taxi as we rode to the Bed and Breakfast, where we would stay during our first visit to Durban.

We stopped briefly at the B&B to refresh ourselves then headed straight out to dinner. Although dog-tired and weary from our travels, dinner at the restaurant in the Protea Hotel Edward promised to be the most exciting part yet of a very long day.

The restaurant was sparsely populated. In fact, there were only a few other tables with patrons and so there was an unexpected quiet to the place, given the size of the room.

About a dozen of us were gathered in the restaurant for this event. Half of us were from Georgia State University (GSU), half from Durban University of Technology (DUT). GSU faculty members were there at the invitation of DUT to talk about shared interests in promoting global awareness of the educational needs of our respective students. I was there to consult with those educators who worked with deaf and hard-of-hearing learners. My Associate Dean, Dr. Gwen Benson, was there at the invitation of Ms. Gandhi, who as it turned out, was Chancellor of DUT. Introductions were made. Small talk ensued. We were ushered to a large table.

"This is the table where Queen Elizabeth dined on her recent visit to Durban," said Dr. Lavern Samuels. Lavern was coordinator of DUT's international programs. He was our host for the evening. "In fact, this is the very chair where she sat." He gestured at a chair at the end of the table, somewhat more ornate than the rest.

The giggly little girl in me wanted to sit in the Queen's chair just to say I had. The adult in me felt it would be intrusive given the formality of the situation.

Now Susan, mind your manners. Control yourself. We can sit on the Queen's throne another time. This isn't it.

After a few more minutes, Lavern invited us to take our seats. "The plan for this evening," he said, "is to move seats between courses so everyone will have a chance to exchange conversation with Ms. Gandhi."

He motioned for me to sit at the end of the table near Ela—she at the proper end, and I in the first seat diagonally to her right. Seated to her left and across from me was Dr. Gwen Benson. Dr. Susan "Sue" Ogletree, Director of the Education Research Bureau, sat to Gwen's left. My husband, Dewey Troutman, who was with me on this first trip to South Africa, was seated to my right. Unbeknownst to me, he sat in the Queen's chair. He is bolder than I and was clearly delighted, based on the twinkle in his eyes.

"It is such a pleasure to meet you, Ms. Gandhi," I began. "Gwen has spoken so fondly of you."

She had a slight smile curling at the corners of her mouth, fingers intertwined, elbows on the arms of her chair at the opposite end of the table from Queen Elizabeth's seat.

"I hope she hasn't given you the wrong impression," she said in a soft and whispery voice. "I'm just a person." Slightly high-pitched with a waver, her voice was patient and grandmotherly. She spoke slowly, enunciating distinctly.

"Tell me about yourself? Do you have children?" she asked. She turned in her seat to look at me eye to eye.

"Yes, Ma'am," I said. "I certainly do. This is a favorite topic of mine. My son is one of the most interesting and challenging people I know. He is smart, loving, friendly, and a daredevil. Of course, he is grown now, but as a helicopter pilot he delights in telling me hair-raising stories of near misses."

"Yes, I have two sons myself," she said, "and they were always finding ways to entertain themselves that would challenge me as well. But raising confident and compassionate children is one of the most important things we must do. One of my grandfather's famous quotes is 'It is easier to build a boy than to mend a man.' Many of the world's ills could be prevented if parents would have high expectations for compassionate behavior and would model this behavior themselves."

Her demeanor is as calm and as steady as if she were talking about the weather. I am all aflutter. She just spoke so casually about one of my heroes, the great Mahatma. I guess to her he is just her grandfather, Gandhiji.

The wait staff came around to take our orders. She turned to face our server.

"How are you this evening? Did you have a good day?" she asked.

Her voice was quiet and assured. She used the same friendly tone that she used with everyone.

It's interesting how she positions herself to face each individual, whether professor or waitress, giving her calm and undivided attention to each as if they were the most interesting person in the room. She has such a knack for making everyone feel treasured.

We began examining our menus.

"Oh, Ms. Gandhi," I said. "This doesn't have very many vegetarian options. I know this is a part of your heritage. Perhaps we should have gone to a different restaurant. I hope you'll have enough to eat." My eyes darted around the menu, looking for something to suggest.

"I don't really need much at a meal," she said. She smiled at me politely, lips closed, their corners raised. "And I have always found you can get a potato just about anywhere."

We continued talking about many things, mostly pertaining to our reason for being in South Africa in the first place. She carefully shared her attention with all, asking and answering questions as they were posed.

"Ms. Gandhi," I said, "Listening to all this wonderful conversation about your life and experiences, the challenges you faced, and the work you continue to do today, have you written an autobiography? I would love to read it. I am sure it would be interesting and inspirational."

"Oh no," she said. "I wouldn't know what to say. And I have not done anything other people far more well-known than I have done. There are so many people with accomplishments on a far grander scale."

Let's tuck this notion in the back of your head for later examination.

The group retired from the table and moved to the penthouse for postprandial conversation. After we were seated, Lavern spoke.

"Our original plan was to invite you to my home tomorrow evening for a traditional homemade Indian dinner. On the elevator ride up, Ela said she would like to invite you to her flat and prepare you a meal."

"Oh, how sweet of you," said Sue. She turned to me and raised her eyebrows in approval.

"That is very kind," said Dr. Hayward Richardson. Hayward was a

Clinical Assistant Professor in the Education Administration Program at GSU. His wife, Janice, a nurse, was with us.

This is an unexpected pleasure.

In the lounge, I sat next to Lavern. I made my move. "Do you have any suggestions for how I might take a basket to the Zulu King?" He looked at me with eyes wide open in surprise but then regained his composure and took on an air of patience. I could see he was weighing his answer.

He thinks I am nuts. I described the basket and my purpose.

"It is highly unlikely we could arrange this," he said. "It takes months to get an audience with the King."

"But I don't have months" I said. I must have looked crestfallen. "I will see if we can sort it out for you," he said. He turned to converse with Gwen.

My husband sat beside Ela. I was beside him.

"Do you like spicy foods?" she asked us. "I have simple tastes because we were raised on simple foods grown at the Phoenix Settlement. Times were difficult back then and you had to make do with what you had. We considered some rice and a few vegetables to be a good meal. I shall make some of them for you for tomorrow's dinner."

A personal invitation to dinner at the home of Ela Gandhi. I did not expect this.

The hour was late, our day long. It was time to end the evening. As we rose from our seats to leave, Dewey pulled out his camera.

"Ms. Gandhi," he said. "Would you mind if Susan took my picture with you?"

She agreed. She folded one hand over the other in preparation.

"I bet you wish you had a dollar for every time someone asked for a picture with you," Dewey said.

"I wish I were more pleasing to look at to make their pictures more worthwhile. And please call me Ela."

That is when his heart melted.

Returning to our lodgings after dinner, we passed through a keyed, double-doored entryway. The house, cottages, and outbuildings of the complex were fortified with barbed wire atop very high walls. The security of the place and of all the homes and buildings we saw on our drives to and from the restaurant caused my homebody self to have one exciting and simultaneously disquieting thought.

This is going to be a very different experience.

From Atlanta to Durban to a dinner invitation from Ela Gandhi to this fortress that became our home away from home, it promised to be very different indeed.

Chapter 2

Lessons in Culture

Waking up the next morning I was a bit disoriented. Perhaps it was the jetlag, or maybe I was unaccustomed to the warmth of the South African summer, heavy with a musky humidity from the Indian Ocean. No matter the reason, it took me a few moments to register I was not waking in my own bed at home on Lake Lanier in Georgia. The plane trip took its toll on my 60-year-old body and it complained to me as I stretched and crawled out of bed.

My colleague, Sue, was rooming in the adjacent cottage. "Time to get going." She sang this in her always up-beat, cheery voice. "Breakfast."

Sitting at the communal picnic table outside the guest quarters, we shared warm, fragrant cups of coffee. Soon other members of our group, Hayward, Janice, and Gwen joined us with mugs of their own.

Gwen steered the conversation from a discussion of our accommodations to information about our plans for the day. "In about 45 minutes, Strini is coming to pick us up." She was standing beside the picnic table, one knee resting on the bench. Dr. Strini Pillay, a member of Durban University of Technology's (DUT) Department of Public Management and Economics, became good friends with Gwen and Sue on their previous visit to Durban. "Better get a move on," she said.

"We're in for an interesting day," I said to Dewey, as each pair in the group walked to our separate quarters. Morning ablutions were in order. As planned, Strini picked us up about an hour later.

"This way," he said. He led us to the exit of the compound to leave our B & B. Our hostess unlocked the first door, and we walked into the vestibule. She locked it behind us then unlocked the door exiting to the street.

"Enjoy your day," she said. She closed the door behind us quickly, retreating into the compound.

We encountered this double layer of protection from intruders in many places throughout the city. Years of violence, death, and destruction at the hands of the apartheid and anti-apartheid violence engendered a gut-level, enculturated response to personal safety. Even now, about 15 years later, the sense of uneasiness was palpable.

"Hurry to the van, please," Strini said. He had some urgency in his voice.

Crowding into the van, we sat elbow to elbow, knee to knee, all six of us taller and larger than most of the slender, shorter South Africans we met. We rode this way for several miles to DUT.

At DUT we were led to a lecture arena for our morning presentations. Our first task of the trip was to present lectures on strategies to impact the future of education. Thirty plus school principals, assistant principals, professors, teachers, and interpreters sat in the auditorium. Hayward and I began with the morning sessions; his on educational leadership, mine on the importance of addressing child variance. Janice and Dewey sat in the back row, taking in the experience.

Naively I attempted to make a connection with the audience, comparing problems in the U.S. to those in South Africa.

"We, too, have a challenge to serve the educational needs of our ever-growing homeless population living in over-crowded shelters," I said.

A woman in the audience raised her hand.

"Yes?" I said. I motioned her to stand.

"You have shelters for your homeless people?" she said. Her voice rose in disbelief. "Then why do you call them homeless?"

Kablam. First awakening. Homeless in South Africa clearly means something different from what it means in the US. I was trying to show solidarity. Instead I just embarrassed myself. Your cultural privilege is showing.

"Homeless shelters provide food, showers, and a place to sleep for the night," I said. My cheeks felt flushed. I tried to talk my way out of the blunder. "They are not permanent residences."

They aren't buying this.

During the luncheon break we had an opportunity to listen to the participants' concerns. Some were the same as ours, but most were issues we could not fathom. One principal of a school for the deaf described a common scene.

"When I arrive at the gates of the school," he said, "often I will find a little deaf child of 3 or 4 years sitting in the dirt, crying, no language, no note saying who his parents are, no possessions other than some food in a paper bag."

Shocking.

Another teacher explained how difficult it had been for her to learn to teach deaf children. "We have no certification programs in deafness in this province," she said. "I had to go to London to receive my training. I have never had a teacher's aide who knew sign language. Many times, my children's deaf grandmothers will come to school with them. They will sit outside and look through the windows, watching me teach. They are thrilled to learn sign language and to be able to talk with their grandchildren."

I could weep right here and now.

"What a wonderful service you are providing," I said. "You are forging an important connection between the children and their grandmothers."

What a fraud. I have no real solutions to offer for such dire circumstances.

When the luncheon was served, I was introduced to a wonderful dish I had not experienced before–the samosa. I turned to the woman manning the table. She wore a crisp, white uniform.

"What is a samosa?" I put one on my plate, then picked it up by its crusty edges and turned it over and over, as if examining a puzzle piece.

"A samosa is a flaky, triangular shell filled with a variety of spicy or savory items," she said. "Perhaps mashed boiled potatoes, or onions with peas and lentils. The pastry is deep-fried to a golden-brown and eaten with chutney or mint or other sauces. Or they may be sweet and filled with fruits or vegetables." She pointed out the different varieties of samosas and sauces as she explained them to me.

Second cultural awakening.

"Oh, my goodness," I said. The juice of a savory lentil samosa dripped down my chin. "This is my new favorite food." It smelled of spices and oil.

Back in the auditorium for the afternoon sessions, Dewey, Janice, and I sat in the rear seats. Mine creaked as I sat down.

In my 40 plus years of doing this, Dewey has never seen me on the job. Doing my thing.

"Well," I said to Dewey. "What did you think of my presentation this morning?"

"Very good." He was shaking out his knees after sitting for half a day.

Odd. On any other topic he is far from being a man of a few words.

Gwen led the next set of conversation on strategies for creating educational partnerships. Sue conducted a workshop on grant proposal writing. This gave me a chance to observe the crowd. They were dressed in everything from modern, western clothing to exotic eastern clothing. All were well-spoken and articulate. Their questions showed a level of quick thinking and deeper comprehension.

Riding back to the B&B, we were mostly quiet, tired from standing for long stretches of the day and engaging in challenging and interesting conversations. Out of the car, through the first locked door, into the vestibule, locking door one, unlocking door two, and safely into the compound, we started on our separate ways toward our bungalows.

"You have 90 minutes to get ready to go to Ela's for dinner," said

Gwen. "Let's gather at the picnic table about 10 minutes before. See you in 80."

I cannot tell a lie. Jet lag and the stress of standing in front of an unknown audience took their toll. I slept hard for 60 of those minutes until Dewey shook me awake.

Flying. A giant samosa whizzes by. Wait, what? I struggled against the urge to fall back to sleep, slowly crawling my way back to full consciousness.

"I hope you know what you're wearing because you have 20 minutes to get ready," he said. I flew through my suitcase, dressing in record time.

Gathered outside the bungalows, Gwen said, "Half of us are riding to Ela's in Strini's van. The other half is going with Professor Nqabomzi Gawe. She is the Acting Chancellor of DUT. Be sure to ask Dr. Gawe to pronounce her first name for you because I can't do it," said Gwen. "The first part of her name is said with a clicking sound. Several of the consonants in the Zulu language incorporate clicks."

Next cultural awakening.

Like silly little school children, we all tried making clicking noises, laughing at one another until our rides arrived. Then back out the first locked door, into the vestibule, locking the first door, un-locking the second, and out in the street we went.

This process must get tiring.

"Hurry to the car, please," said Strini and Dr. Gawe. They both surveilled the area as we walked in single file to the cars.

Driving through Durban on the way to Ela's flat, we agreed with the travel brochures telling us it is a little jewel of a city on the southeastern coast of the African continent looking out upon the Indian Ocean.

Sue read the brochure, using her best imitation of a radio an-nouncer. "Small by comparison to many cities," she said, "the metropolitan region is home to around 3.5 million residents. Durban has a subtropical climate and is bordered by extensive, sugary beaches. In addition to its original African inhabitants, 24% of the population are of Indian/Asian descent, forming the largest population of residents of Indian heritage outside of India."

Didn't realize the significance of the cultural mix 'til this trip. Next cultural awakening.

"In fact," she said, "there are 11 different official languages in South Africa. Most citizens of the country know at least two."

U.S. kids are at such a disadvantage knowing only English. Cultural deficit.

Sue's voice trailed off. The Indian ocean came into view, and we all stared. It was vast and active. Substantial waves washed the shoreline. An impressive sight.

The information from the brochure occupied my mind as we travelled through the city and up a hill toward Ela's flat. Exiting Strini's car, I finally met Dr. Gawe.

"Hello, I am Nqabomzi Gawe."

There it was. That click. As we walked up the stairs to the elevator, which would take us to Ela's flat, I couldn't wait to find an appropriate time to ask for a lesson in pronouncing her name.

Chapter 3

Dinner at Ela's

Ela's flat was in a high-rise building across town from our B&B. Stepping off the elevator, we turned down a long hallway with lovely wooden facades on many of the doors. Ela opened the entryway to her home and beckoned us in.

"Welcome," she said, "Do come in." A warm, spicy aroma emanated from the doorway.

The layout of the flat was compact and comfortable. A small kitchen to the left, bedrooms and facilities were to the right. Straight ahead was a large dining table, enough to seat Ela, Lavern, Dr. Gawe, and our party of six. Six straight-backed, wooden chairs covered in tastefully designed blue and rose fabric surrounded a maple wood table. A few stray chairs commandeered from other parts of the home finished the ensemble. Beyond the kitchen and dining room, to the left, we entered Ela's living room.

"Wow," I said. My eyes could not take it all in.

"Oh, my," Sue and Gwen said. Hushed tones felt appropriate.

"Extraordinary," another of our group said. We had entered her personal museum of Gandhi history.

"Would you mind giving us a tour?" Dewey asked. "So interesting."

We began at the piano over which hung a large portrait of her grandfather, Mohandas Karamchand Gandhi. This portrait dominated the room. You could almost feel his presence. To the right of his picture was a lovely portrait all in red tones. "An art student at DUT painted it for me," she said.

Ela pointed at the picture to the left of her grandfather. "My mother painted this picture," she said. "It is a picture of Krishna. I cherish this picture because my mother created it so painstakingly.

When I look at it, I see Krishna and I see my mother." Respect, love, pride, and a hint of longing all intermingled in her voice. For a moment, her eyes seemed far away, then in an instant she was back and resumed the tour.

Next, she called attention to some pictures of other family members. "These are my children," she said. "And this is my son. He is late," she said in a lowered voice.

I am embarrassed to admit I almost made a linguistic blunder, assuming the term, "late" referred to time, but then realized she was referring to her late son. "Oh," I said. Compassion based in personal loss was in my voice. "I am sorry for your loss. It's not easy to lose someone so cherished. I lost my sister recently."

Well that's graceless, Susan. It's not about your loss, it's about hers.

"Losing a child is just about the worst shock a mother can experience," I said. I put my arm around her shoulder and gave her a little hug. She smiled, comforting me rather than me comforting her.

We moved on to other artifacts in the room. Credenzas, bookshelves, cupboards with glass doors, and display cases covered every available wall space. From busts of Gandhi, to photos of Ela with the Dalai Lama, or Mandela, or the Pope, to African artifacts, to religious artifacts, there were captivating objects of her rich personal history everywhere.

Dewey was snapping away with his camera.

"You may take any pictures you wish," she said, "but I prefer you not take pictures of my awards. They are personal." We complied.

Two artifacts fascinated me. One was a pair of Gandhi's glasses.

A new city, new country, new continent, new hemisphere, and I'm looking at the Mahatma's glasses. Extraordinary.

The other item was a hand-made wooden spoon. I am the present custodian of an abundance of spoons, which have come down to me through six generations of family. A responsibility I hold dear.

Ask Ela about the spoon. Has to be a story behind it.

I was about to ask her for the story, but she excused herself, so I filed this thought away for future reference.

"I must go attend to our dinner," she said, "or you will be hungry tonight."

"Is there anything I can do to help you?" just about everyone in the room asked.

"Thank you, no," she answered. "It is a small kitchen. Easier to make final preparations myself."

As we were wandering around, pointing out compelling artifacts to one another, I positioned myself near Dr. Gawe. There were two items on my agenda.

"Dr. Gawe," I said, "Gwen suggested I ask you about the pronunciation of your first name. I understand that clicks are phonetic devices in the local language. Is it difficult to learn?"

"No, not at all difficult if you learn it from your family as a baby. But you might struggle with it." She smiled and we all chuckled.

"There are several clicks in IsiXhosa," she explained. "A different letter represents each. The q in my name, Nqabomzi, is produced with a 'tock' sound at the top and front of the palate."

We tried to imitate her. None of us was successful.

"Another click is made with the side of the tongue against the side teeth, like the sound you make to inspire a horse."

We tried again. We failed again.

"The next one is made with the tip of the tongue inside the front teeth. This is like the tsk tsk sound people make waving their finger at a naughty child."

Once again, no success. But it was a valuable first lesson.

The second item on my agenda was the basket.

"Dr. Gawe," I said. I avoided her first name. "Do you have any suggestions for how I might arrange an audience with His Majesty, King Goodwill Zwelithini kaBekuzulu?" I practiced his name on the plane ride over. I explained the situation with the basket. She paused, considering her response.

"You see," she said, "a meeting of this nature would take months to arrange." Carefully, patiently, and apologetically she explained the difficulty inherent in my question. "It is highly irregular and most likely an impossible request. It would be required to have your request granted through a series of lesser chiefs and offices before anyone would consider presenting it to the King."

Another cultural lesson.

"But I don't have months," I said. "I have only days." I repeated the plea I made to Lavern the day before. As had Lavern, she promised to do what she could. "Thank you for any help you can give me," I said. I tried to keep my disappointment in check.

I snapped out of my petulance when Ela came out of the kitchen and declared, "Dinner is served." She invited us to seat ourselves. We all moved toward the table, filtering into the seats as we attempted to give deference to Dr. Gawe and our hostess.

"Would you like some Chai Tea?" Ela asked. Most of us accepted.

"Do you have any regular tea?" Dewey said.

"I shall make some," said Ela. She left the room again to make the tea while Sue poured cups of Chai for the rest of us.

After having a taste of my warm, fragrant, spicy Chai Tea, Dewey leaned closer so he could whisper to me. "I wish I had said yes to the Chai," he said, eyeing my tea.

Maybe next time. This is mine.

Dinner was a lovely mix of dishes. There were potatoes, rice, rolls, vegetables, lentils, and semolina pudding.

"Ela, this is the best semolina pudding I have ever tasted," I said.

Tell the truth. It's the only semolina pudding you've ever tasted. Worth the long hours of torture by airplane.

After dinner, we sat around the table, talking and sharing stories. The conversation turned to struggles during the Apartheid years.

"Ela," Janice said. "We lived through violence in the South during the Civil Rights movement. I remember those fearful times. You suffered so many hardships during Apartheid. We were often afraid. What did you do when fear became too much for you?"

Ela thought for a moment and then relayed a personal story.

"Once during the worst of Apartheid and our anti-Apartheid efforts, I was arrested. We were protesting the cost of rent. The police came to our protest. They set upon all of us, pushing and shoving,

Counterclockwise from left front—Gwen, Susan, Lavern, Sue, Ela, Janice, Hayward, Nqabomzi

hit some with their clubs. Many were crying and screaming. Then they threw us violently into the back of their jail van. We were crowded tightly. There wasn't room enough for everyone to sit. Some of us were on the floor. We were packed tightly."

She says this so calmly.

"I am claustrophobic. My claustrophobia compounded my fear from the violence of the arrest."

I'll bet.

"People were crying and moaning all around me," she said. "There was nothing for me to do."

She paused, becoming very quiet.

"What did you do?" several people asked, almost in unison.

"I have heard it said, 'Nothing is softer or more flexible than water, yet nothing can resist it.' This calmed me and I began to sing, 'We Shall Overcome.' One by one the others in the van began to sing as well. By the time we arrived at the police station, we felt calmer."

Music hath the charm.

"Panic is a dangerous emotion," she said. "Calm can quell panic. Panic led the soldiers to attack the participants in Gandhiji's Salt March in India. Panic can lead to more harm than the actual incident itself. So, I decided to stop panicking."

Did not think of it as a choice. A brave choice.

"I was arrested many times," Ela said. "Once we protested against the Home Affairs department. Home Affairs issued identity documents for people. Now, we were going toward the first democratic elections and this department was refusing to provide identity documents for people who had no other papers. There are so many people in this country whose documents were confiscated, who had the previous dompasses. There was so much violence; warehouses of documents were burned. And there were so many reasons why people didn't have legitimate documents. By not giving the people documents, all these people would not be able to vote."

Voter suppression—a common tactic to this day.

"So, we marched to the Home Affairs offices and just sat there quietly," she said. "Occupied the place. This happened all over the country. They tried to make us leave but we said, 'No, get us assurances that everyone will be able to register and then we will leave.' This time the police were a little more polite. I think it was 1993, just before the 1994 elections, and I think they had learned to be more polite. This time the van had seats."

Well that's a step in the right direction, although a small comfort.

"Again, we were in a huge police cell where we sat for the whole day. The person who is now our minister of police, Beiki Cele, came there to release us, and there was a huge gate which you open with a remote control. The police had just opened the gate and Mr. Cele was ducking his head in and we saw that the gate was going to come straight down crashing on his head."

Frightening and intimidating.

"We screamed and fortunately he withdrew because otherwise he would have been dead," she said. "We think that was deliberately done but we can't prove it. It was a terrible experience just to see it. He had come to release us and almost lost his life. He is now the minister of police in South Africa. He recalls this experience as well."

We sat quietly, lost for a while in our own thoughts.

Then Ela said, "Would you care for some dessert?" She stood and headed toward the kitchen.

Ela is not one to linger on the past, or on painful thoughts. I have heard it said, "If you don't like what you are thinking, change your mind." That soft approach is one of her greatest strengths.

Chapter 4

The Phoenix Settlement

My husband and I elected to take a tour of the Phoenix Settlement the next day. After breakfast our driver arrived in a modest yet comfortable car. A large man, he was quiet in nature. Once again, we exited the first locked door, walked into the vestibule, locked it, then unlocked the door exiting to the street, a double layer of protection from intruders, now familiar in many places throughout the city.

"Hurry, please." Our driver watched the street carefully, encouraging us not to dawdle. In we crawled, finally feeling less sore from the earlier journey than the day before.

"Phoenix Settlement, please," we said.

"Yes ma'am. I have been told," the driver replied.

As we rode past rolling hills of green and brown clumps of thick, tall grass, I was impressed by the modern highways leading out of Durban.

This doesn't look so very different from some of the subtropical parts of the US I have visited.

No sooner had this thought entered my head than I spied one glaring exception. A brightly colored flashing sign pointed us in an alternate direction, beckoning us to visit the Zululand Casino and Entertainment Kingdom.

Totally unexpected. I'm pondering Gandhi, humanity, and the higher purpose of life. My eyes are enticed by roulette wheels, craps tables, and one-armed bandits.

Half an hour later, down various paved roads, we passed informal housing, where a mother washed her child's hair by the side of the road, rinsing dirt and grime with a pan of hose water onto the street.

Arriving at the historic site of the old Phoenix Settlement, we were eagerly greeted by some schoolboys returning home for the day.

"Hallo," they shouted. "Who are you? Where are you from? What are you doing here?" they asked. They peppered us with questions.

"We're from Georgia in the United States," Dewey answered. "Do you live around here?"

"Yes," they said. They waved their arms in the general direction of the informal housing surrounding the heritage campus of the Settlement.

"Did you enjoy school today?" I asked. And then, ever the teacher, "What did you learn about?"

"We had maths and science today," they answered. They passed by, giggling and buzzing with the social subtext of the day.

Maths? A new expression to me, but it makes sense. Math isn't just one thing. It's numerals, addition, fractions, geometry, calculus, and so on, so "maths" it is.

Informal Housing at the Settlement

Our large yet quiet driver directed us to the young Indian man who would be our tour guide. Short in stature with thin, light features, he greeted us.

"Hello," he said. "Ela informed me you would be coming to visit. It would be my pleasure to show you around."

"We're in luck," Dewey said. He nudged me with his elbow.

"Really," I said. "I wouldn't have known where to begin. How sweet of Ela to think of us like this."

Our guide began his program.

"Mohandas Gandhi was born in India on October 2nd of 1869. His family followed the Vaishnava faith, although his mother was a devout follower of the Jain tradition. This religion encouraged compassion for all beings, vegetarianism, fasting for self-purification, and mutual tolerance between individuals of different creeds."

"I can see how his early experiences helped to shape his beliefs," I said.

"Yes," Dewey echoed. "When I was in college, we read that he used fasting as a tool for social protest. He fasted as a protest against British rule of India, right?" he asked our guide.

"Yes. That is correct."

"Gandhi was trained as an attorney at the University College of London," our guide said.

Our conversation was interrupted by another wave of school children walking past the heritage site. They laughed, teased, and pushed one another, clearly glad to be released from school.

"I read somewhere that Gandhi was a voracious reader. Everything from the Bhavagad Gita and the Bible to Tolstoy. He even studied with members of London's Theosophical Society for a while," I said.

"Yes, that is correct," said our guide. "You must have been speaking with Ela."

"No," I said.

I have read about Theosophy myself and his philosophy matches theirs. Especially his philosophy that we all are one.

"I hope I get a chance to ask Ela about this."

There's that thought again. Gotta encourage Ela to write her autobiography.

The guide continued his program as we slowly walked the grounds.

"Gandhi came to South Africa to practice law in 1893. He planned to remain for one year but did not return to India until 1924, twenty-one years later. He suffered insults, injuries, and outrageous treatment, which ignited his desire for social justice. On a train ride to Pretoria, he was kicked off the train in Pietermaritzburg because of his race, even though he had purchased a first-class ticket."

Oh, yeah. I saw that in the Gandhi movie we watched before we came here.

"He was beaten and jailed on several occasions," said our guide. "These injustices caused him to choose South Africa as the place to stand and fight racial discrimination."

We passed several plaques and signs along the way, and our guide stopped to explain them.

He said, "Gandhi built the Settlement upon a 3-pronged philosophy: Satyagraha, Ahimsa, & Sarvodaya. Satyagraha means non-violence based on the force of truth. Ahimsa means truth and Sarvodaya means the progress or welfare of all. Phoenix was his first ashram and the Settlement was devoted to living a principled life based on these three prongs. He even named his home, Sarvodaya."

My mind started to wander. Through history there have been great men and women who fought against discrimination. Gandhi, Martin Luther King, Ela years later in South Africa, and the list goes on.

What would it take to make a permanent change in human nature? I would love to know what Ela thinks about this.

The tour continued. We were at the printing house.

"Gandhi first published *The Indian Opinion* in 1903 to support the struggle against racial discrimination and for civil rights. Its purpose," said our guide, "was to highlight the struggles of South African Indians and South African Blacks. These groups were not permitted to tell their own stories in the newspapers of the day. Such a thing was not allowed. But Gandhi set about to change that."

"Well, he sure put his heart and soul into it," Dewey said. "He is the face of so many efforts in so many countries."

"Yes," agreed our guide. He seemed ready to move our tour along.

"The settlers built the original building to house a small school," he said. "But the government built a school nearby and the decision was made to close the Settlement school. By that time, Gandhi's son, Manilal, was running the settlement. He decided to move the printing press into the old school building. Later, when that building rotted, he moved the press into the building that exists on the grounds today."

"Is the paper still printed in this building?" I asked.

"No," he said. "Manilal Gandhi kept the presses running until 1956, when he died of a stroke. His wife, Sushila, took over, managing the Settlement, the Press, and the weekly newspaper until 1962. The Apartheid government at that time imposed stringent restrictions on the media, silencing the presses altogether."

"So," I said, "that means in the 34 years from 1962 until the end of Apartheid in 1996, the Indian and Black communities were barred from publishing any anti-Apartheid sentiments in the established media. Is that correct?" He nodded in agreement.

Moving on, we crossed the pathway from the press to the Gandhi museum. Along the way, we saw busts and statues of Mohandas Gandhi, as well as various small buildings with plaques providing descriptions and information.

Inside the museum there were pictures of Gandhi, testaments from other famous individuals of the impact the man had on the world, and lecture rooms where members of the settlement could plan

Original Press Building

Original Press

New Printing House, 1940

and implement community activism and reform. There was also a small, empty room with an ancient-looking dentist's chair and equipment. Today, dentists from Durban volunteer their time to provide dental care to the residents of the Settlement.

"Gandhi was very active," said our guide, "initiating legal actions, organizing the community to protest injustices, providing leadership to the Phoenix community, and establishing the Natal Indian Congress. He organized the Natal Indian Ambulance Corps and was a stretcher carrier during the 1906 Zulu rebellion against British rule and taxation."

I didn't know that.

"He suffered many jailings as a result of these and other activities," said our guide.

Our last stop on the tour was the site of Sarvodaya, Gandhi's original home on the Settlement.

"During the Apartheid government's actions to remove Black and Indian South Africans from areas desired by Whites," said our guide, "the home was burned to the ground. Violence against non-whites in South Africa occurred routinely up until the end of Apartheid in 1996."

It was quite sobering to stand on the same spot where the great Mahatma sat, rocking in his chair in the gentle breeze, overlooking hill after hill after hill of informal housing.

We could almost feel the love, warmth, support, and mutual respect that Settlement dwellers must have experienced. I hoped I would have a chance to ask Ela what it was like growing up in such a unique environment.

Dewey at Rebuilt Gandhi Home, Sarvodaya

View from the Front Porch

Chapter 5

The Zulu Restaurant

Indian cuisine one night, Zulu cuisine the next. Tonight, we would be going to a restaurant on the boardwalk by the ocean for an authentic Zulu meal. This truly was an international city.

We returned from our trip to the Phoenix Settlement through the intricate entryway. Sue and Gwen were seated at the picnic table again, having returned from their day's work at DUT.

"So, what did you think about the Settlement?" Sue asked. "Pretty interesting, wasn't it?"

"You can say that again," I said. "It was a beautiful day to experience such history and culture." Our minds were full of sights and scenes from the Settlement and we couldn't wait to share our experiences with the rest of the traveling group.

"Do you know when Ela was born?" I asked Sue. I sat down at the table, one leg over the bench as if riding a horse.

"I think she said in 1940." She turned to me as if expecting further information.

"The guide told us her dad, Manilal, died in 1956," I said. "That would have made her 16 when he died. This makes me sad."

Reminds me of my niece. She lost her mother, my sister, when she was 13. Loss is a struggle. Poor 16-year-old Ela.

"It would have been hard enough to grow up in such a volatile country" I said. "Then to lose your father, who was also the leader of the community you lived in would be a challenge for any teenager."

My thoughts were still with my niece.

Manilal and Sushila

Sita

Ela and Arun

"Sushila, her mom, was a strong woman, though," Sue said, "and Ela had an older sister and brother to turn to." A stray cloud passed overhead. I covered my eyes with my hand and looked up for a moment.

"What were their names?" I asked.

"The sister is Sita and the brother is Arun," Sue said. "Arun was about 6 years older and Sita was about 12 years older."

"Yes, but it's not the same as having a father then losing him before you are even grown," I said. I shook my head ruefully.

"But it happens all the time, especially in marginalized communities," said Sue. "The HIV epidemic caused havoc in Africa. Add poor nutrition, lack of healthcare, all those sorts of things. And then the violence this country went through. It's always the children who suffer the most."

"Yes," I said. "The most vulnerable always take the heat."

I wonder how Ela dealt with it.

"Anyway." she said. She stood up from the picnic table. "You can ask her about it at dinner tonight. She'll be at the restaurant."

We went to our individual cottages to get ready for dinner. The five-year-old son of the B&B owners peeked one eye around the corner of the open doorway to the main house and I winked at him. He scooted back inside.

He's a very lucky boy to be born in this decade in South Africa and not before.

We wandered between the picnic table and bungalows, each person with his own agenda, waiting for Strini to pick us up at the appointed time.

He walked in.

"Yes," he said into his phone. "We're leaving just now." He walked over and sat down at the picnic table, apparently in no hurry.

That phrase appeals to the linguist in me. His use of "just now" seems unusually timed. Must be another one of those South African expressions. We say, "traffic light." They say, "robot." They say "scheme" and mean "a plan." We say "scheme" and think it's something nefarious.

"Strini," I asked. "Are we leaving now?"

"Yes," he said, "Just now." He turned to Gwen and continued his conversation.

OK, I guess it means 'soon.' And soon we did leave.

We parked in the designated lot at the boardwalk on the Indian Ocean. We could instantly see why it was given the name, "The Golden Mile." A mile-long brick promenade running from the Suncoast Casino to uShaka beach wended its way past hotels, pools, restaurants, and shops of all kinds. Women in colorful native garb set out their wares on tables and blankets. A variety of jewelry, masks, scarves, and trinkets was arrayed neatly. Stone and wood carvings of "The Big Five," lions, black rhinos, elephants, leopards, and Cape buffaloes tempted me.

As if these colorful and unique options were not enough of a feast for the eyes, the beachside of the promenade was edged with all manner of sand sculptures. Intricate in detail, these sculptures rivaled any I had seen on other beaches. There were lions, monkeys, fish scenes, castles, warriors, and kings. The level of creativity was impressive.

Our restaurant was in the uShaka Village at the end of the boardwalk. The décor was not unlike any beachside restaurant you might find, with one exception. The waiters and waitresses were dressed in striking orange and red outfits. Miniskirts and tops with beaded necklaces on the women, the men in longer skirts with leopard print tops. Throughout the meal they would stop and perform a Zulu dance.

In addition to our regular group, Ela, Lavern, Strini and his wife, and Nan Kanaye dined with us. Nan, the director of services for deaf and hard-of-hearing students at DUT, was dressed in a gorgeous, emerald-colored in-saatva, a short-sleeved, knee-length dress. It was stunning against her golden skin.

"So nice to meet you, Nan." I said. "Ela has told me about the work you are doing at DUT."

"Pleasure," said Nan. She spoke softly, drawing out the vowel sound. "And you work with deaf students as well."

"Yes, I do," I said. This was actually the impetus for my visit.

"Have you any deaf children of your own?" she asked. She had a pleasant and polished expression on her face.

"No, but sometimes my son acts as if he doesn't hear a word I say. How about you?" I asked.

"Yes. Two of my children are deaf. That is how I came to be in the field," she said.

"I'm asked that question all the time," I said. "How did I get into the field of deaf education? Did I have a family member who was deaf? My response is always, 'Just lucky, I guess.'"

I have heard it said one has his job in life. This feeds his stomach. And one has his work in life. This feeds his soul. Lucky is the person whose job and work are one and the same.

"Please tell me about your program," I said. "What are the challenges you have?"

We began discussing the issues she was facing at the university.

"Availability of interpreters is always a problem," said Nan. "This is because there are many languages to interpret. I am sure you know there are eleven official languages in South Africa."

"Yes," I said.

Just one official language causes problems among signers in the U.S. Can't imagine the havoc 11 would wreak.

"The variety of languages presents a challenge to teachers and interpreters," Nan said. "Which language do you teach them? Afrikaans signs, British English signs, American English signs, indigenous signs? There are several forms of Zulu sign language."

"Oh my, yes," I said." I can see the problem." We continued discussing access to sign language in KwaZulu Natal.

Before I could get to my next question, an artist came to our table offering to paint traditional Zulu designs on our faces.

"This is so interesting," said Dewey. "We are so lucky to be here."

As the evening wore on, I began chatting with Ela.

"Did you enjoy your tour of the Settlement." She looked at me squarely, a smile in her eyes.

Dewey and Susan

"Yes, I did," I said. "Thank you so much for arranging a tour guide for us. That was unexpected." I patted the back of her hand gently.

"I was not able to go with you myself, and I wanted you to be able to ask questions," she said. She looked at me with open-faced anticipation. By now she knew I always had another question.

"Well, I do have a few more questions, if you don't mind," I said.

She nodded her agreement.

"Our guide mentioned your father passed away when you were around 16 years old." I said. "That must have had a huge impact on you as a teenager."

"Yes," she said. "But my mother was very strong. The benefit of living communally is that there were many people there, my brother, sister, and cousins. We had a village of women and men, all of us looking after one another. I was sad, but I was never alone."

No matter how many people you have around you, the loss is still there. The hole can never be filled.

"Were you born at the Settlement?" I asked.

"Yes," she said. "At some unearthly hour in the night, in the original house where Gandhiji used to live, and in the middle of the war years. It is the same house where all my children were born."

"You mean, Sarvodaya," I said.

"Yes." She acknowledged with a gracious nod.

"What was it like growing up at the Settlement?" I was very curious about this after our tour.

"The Phoenix Settlement was a unique experiment Gandhiji established. It was inspired by his visit to the monastery, Mariannehill. There he was impressed with the simple lives of all the different race groups; men and women, sharing the work and living together in simplicity and harmony." The breeze from the Indian Ocean was starting to cool without the sun in the sky.

"Growing up at the Phoenix Settlement afforded me a unique perspective because all Gandhi's ideas and ideals were in practice," Ela said "He passed them down to my parents, and they to me. We had a tradition of equality, respect for labor, and self-sufficiency."

Such a unique upbringing. Too bad all children aren't raised in such a nurturing way.

"My grandfather, and then my parents, felt strongly that one should take just enough to survive and to enjoy life. The minute you take more than you need, you are depriving somebody else," she said.

An important principle that many people overlook.

Lavern was sitting across from us, conversing with Dewey. When he heard the conversation, he turned to us.

"I can attest to that," he said. "Ela is not materially attached to items and if you have a need for something she has, she will gladly share it with you or give it to you."

"'Twas a very principled life," she said. Her voice trailed off as she looked out at the ocean through the restaurant window.

After dinner we headed back out to the promenade, where we stopped to watch a group of young South Africans perform one of their heritage dances. Dressed in skins and feathers, they presented yet another visual feast for the eyes. Drums beat loudly. Voices intoned chants sung for generations. Heads swayed and bodies gyrated to the distinctly Zulu beat. The spectators clapped along with the beat. Many of those in attendance joined in, dancing along with the performers. The performance ended and we continued our stroll.

"Do you have any other questions for me?" Ela asked.

"Well, yes, I do," I said. "If you don't mind, I would love to hear more about the newspaper." *My writer-self wants to know more about the process.*

"My parents used to take me to the press every night when I was around three," Ela said. "They had two huge cane chairs, which they put together face to face and put a little pillow in between. I used to make a little cot when I got tired and sleep in that, and then they would bring me home."

"What a sweet memory," I said. "I can just picture you wiggling around on that cot." She smiled. Images of my son at three years of age popped into my head. We stopped for a moment to admire one of the sand sculptures.

"Every Friday morning," she said, "parcels of newspapers would be taken to the Post Office, and then all the letters of the alphabet would be returned to their individual slots in a huge wooden tray housing the alphabets."

"This is where the concept of upper case and lower case came from, right?" I said. "Capital letters were in the upper trays or cases and regular letters were in the lower case?" Ela acknowledged my interruption with a gracious nod.

"This was like a big typewriter where the people setting the types would be able to know exactly where each alphabet was housed. They would be able to set the types as they read the text which would stand on a wooden stand similar to the piano score holder. Then the whole process, would start anew. They would gather stories on little slips of paper, then organize the news, then set the type and so it went on and on, week after week." She absent-mindedly pantomimed the actions of moving around the letters with her graceful hands.

"When I grew older, I had the task of wrapping the papers into little brown sheets and addressing 900 to 1000 of them by hand. We rolled the newspaper into these. The printing process from start to finish took the entire night. It was very time-consuming."

We continued our stroll along the promenade, enjoying the breeze off the ocean. This breeze came with a mildly unpleasant scent, nothing we couldn't live with. I had heard that there were shark nets not too far offshore to protect anyone brave enough to enter the turbulent water. Perhaps this was why I had not seen anyone dipping their toes into the wild and salty waves.

"Ela," I said. "Other than the press, what are some of your earliest memories of growing up on the Settlement?"

"There are so many," she said. Her eyes looked upwards and to the side, as if she were sorting through many options.

"Because of food shortages related to the austerity brought on by war, some of my earliest memories are of our staple diet of mealie rice," Ela said. "This is a crudely crushed, bland corn meal and it was not at all as flavorful as regular rice."

"Didn't you have other options?" I said.

I hope I didn't wrinkle my nose at the thought. I probably did. I have rarely had to settle for something I did not like, this due to the cultural privilege in which I was raised. Maybe broccoli or liver as a child, typical foods children reject when their palates are young, but never in my adult life.

"No," she said. "Rice was available on the black market, but my parents refused to support the misery that the black markets passed on to the impoverished and underprivileged. One must sacrifice for what you believe in and not submit to illicit means of getting what you want." Her voice remained calm. *An important principle.*

"That's a hard lesson most people prefer not to learn," I said.

Images of the overflowing aisles of fresh foods at the market where I shop popped into my head.

"This was more than just an inconvenience," she said. Her hand raised as if to gesture wait. "This was an issue of principle. Firstly, that rice was not available to everyone so why should we, the minority, make it available to ourselves. The second thing was that if you support something illegal, you also become guilty."

"You are lucky to have learned that lesson at such a young age," I said.

A second principle she learned growing up on the Settlement. Sacrificing one's wants is more important than greedily indulging oneself to the detriment of others.

"Our actions have a ripple effect on everyone around us."

"Yes," she said. "This principle of sacrifice is one humankind has forgotten. We need only to look at the conspicuous consumption of citizens around the world. The Pacific Trash Vortex is huge and continues to grow, and yet use of plastic has not subsided." In this, her voice never lost its gentle, encouraging tone.

"I couldn't agree with you more," I said. Agitation rose in my voice.

"Overcrowding and under-sanitation are likely to cause plagues," I said. "We are all just at the mercy of the next epidemic. The rise in greenhouse gases is going to affect humanity in ways we can't even predict." It doesn't take much for the activist in me to stir.

"Love for one's fellow man is an attitude that your grandfather and many other great philosophers and great religions espoused." I said. "Surely respecting the environment in which one's fellow man will reside is a part of that philosophy, but in practice, humans struggle to see past their immediate desire and greed."

I really hope I can get to hear more of her stories. They are all quite in line with my personal world view.

"Yes," she said. "One of Gandhiji's well-known sayings is 'The world has enough resources to meet everyone's need but not enough for everyone's greed." I shook my head in agreement.

Soon we reached our parking lot. I could have asked Ela another million questions, but the evening was long, and tomorrow was another day. I would be visiting several schools for the deaf with Nan, and I was looking forward to it. That was, after all, my reason for being in South Africa. Time to head back to our B&B for some shut eye. Plenty to ponder on the way.

Chapter 6

Monkey Business

Curiosity woke me the next morning. I would be going to visit some schools for the deaf. This was part of my reason for being in SA, to address my university's strategic goal to achieve distinction in globalizing the university. Nan picked me up for our visit in her personal car.

"This is very kind of you," I said. "Thank you." I slid into the passenger's seat.

"Pleasure," Nan said, a warm smile on her face.

She headed the car away from the curb. She kept her eyes on the road, a good thing given the heavy morning traffic.

We chatted about the previous evening's dinner. Her smile was tolerant as I talked about the picture I took of my husband's face painting.

We arrived at the first of three schools on our agenda.

"The first school we are visiting today," Nan said, "is the Durban School for the Hearing Impaired. It is a school for deaf and hard of hearing children from ages of 3 up to those ready to leave school around 18 or 21 years of age. The Vocational Training Center is a separate part of the school for the older school leavers. It has programs from early childhood through secondary education." Her voice was stronger than usual.

The building had a brick façade and could have been any school in the US in the 1960s. Yellow school buses rested unoccupied to the left of the building.

"Teenagers and young adults attend this school," she said, "and are learning skills for jobs in the hospitality and service industries." Her tone was higher, happy. This was where she belonged.

We walked up the sidewalk and into the building.

"We will meet with the principal later," Nan said. "I am very familiar with this school, so I will take you on a tour first." She walked briskly down the hallway, peering around doors, smiling and nodding at teachers and students she recognized.

We walked through rooms where some students were learning to work in simulated hotel kitchens. Pans clinked. Warm, sweet fragrances wafted from the ovens.

"Some students are learning custodial skills," said Nan. "Others are learning basic accounting or to become hair stylists and barbers."

Most of the students were South African Black. Only a few were Indian. None was Afrikaner White.

We stopped to exchange pleasantries with a group of seven teens.

I turned to Nan. "Would you please translate for me, Nan. I don't know the local sign system. I'm sure it's quite different from the American Sign Language (ASL) or Signed English (SE) I know."

"Pleasure," she said.

"Very nice work," I said to the students in the kitchen. Nan translated this into the sign language used in the school.

"Thank you. Who you?" they signed. Nan translated the question.

"She is a visitor from the United States," she signed.

Hands and fingers of sign language flew back and forth as they nodded agreement to one another.

Some of the signs are similar but most are different. Good thing Nan is with me.

"You need a haircut," signed one of the students in the stylist program.

"You are probably right," Nan signed for me. "Maybe next time I visit, you will cut my hair. OK?"

The student looked pleased and made another comment. She got a stern look from her instructor, along with a comment Nan did not translate for me. We walked on.

"Before the trade schools came about," said Nan, "deaf people were permitted only to work at menial labor." She folded one hand gracefully into the other.

"That's not unlike many other countries of the world," I said. "Deaf people were considered the property of their masters, much as people of color, and even women were."

I hoped I wasn't talking too much. The building was very quiet. We walked to the other end.

"It's very quiet away from the students," I said. "Deaf kids can be raucously loud when they want to."

"Yeees," Nan said with a long, low vowel. "That is true." She smiled a knowing smile.

I've heard this use of the stretched out yeees before. Happens in slow, low, quiet tones. Used to acknowledge something. It's akin to "can I get an Amen, sistah!"

"In the US, women weren't allowed to have their own credit cards until the 1970s," I said. "I got my first card in 1975. I was 25 and single. My dad offered to sign his permission, but I didn't need it. He was not amused."

Nan kept a gentle smile on her face, acknowledging my comment with a blink of her eyes.

I wonder what the financial situation is like in South Africa. Can Nan get her own credit card? That's too personal. I shouldn't ask her.

Continuing our walk through the halls, we met up with the principal. She escorted us to a break room for refreshments. She was thin and carefully coiffed. Taller than other Indian women I met. Kindly but all business. She offered us some refreshments then expanded on the history of the trade school movement as we snacked on samosas and fruit juice.

"Do the students do your hair for you?" I asked.

Lucky to have a hairdresser right at your job.

"I let them sometimes," she said, "but we have had a few disasters in the past, so I am careful whom I permit to work on my hair."

She spoke in the refined grammar I came to associate with most of the Indian women I met.

"The problem we are facing right now is that there are no trade schools once you are outside of the city." She shook her head. Her brows furrowed.

"This is a real problem," she said, "because it contributes to the flight of our young people away from the rural economy and into the problems of city life." She tilted her head.

"Yes," said Nan. "It is difficult for any student of color to find appropriate job training. That is why we are so fortunate to have a trade school for the deaf students right here in Durban."

She is proud of this offering to the students.

"As you know, I am here with a group from my university," I said to the principal. "I will share your concerns with the group."

The 90-minute planned visit flew, and we needed to move on to the next school.

After a short drive through the croplands, grasslands, and wooded savannahs that surround Durban, we arrived at the parking lot of the KwaVuLindlebe (kwa-voo-lind-leh-bay) School for the Deaf. Green doors were interspersed at equal distances down the walkway in front to the red brick building.

We were still in the car. I unbuckled my seatbelt and turned to Nan.

"Nan, I am fairly well-versed at figuring out the basics of a new language, but this one has me out of my element. What does kwa mean? I have seen it in many places. KwaZulu Natal, and now KwaVuLindlebe."

"It means, 'here is' or 'here you will find,' or 'this place is,'" she said. Her voice was soft and delicate, yet instructive. At times I had to lean in to hear her. This softness appeared common among the women of Indian heritage.

"KwaZulu Natal (KZN)," she said, "means, 'here is the homeplace of the Zulu.' KwaVuLindlebe, would mean something such as, 'here is seen Lindlebe.' The translation varies."

The wing of the school housing the deaf students was located across the breezeway behind a red brick school for children with typical hearing ability, a general education school.

"Why are all the doors closed?" Sweat was beading on my brow.

"It's such a hot day and they have no air conditioning," I said. "As a matter of fact, I haven't seen air conditioning in any of the schools and public buildings I've been in."

Nan nodded without comment.

Another blaringly clear example of my cultural privilege.

"The teachers close the doors when children are eating their snacks," she said. Her lips were slightly pursed. "It is a wise idea so the monkeys will not steal their food."

So different.

The principal escorted us around the school. She was shorter than I, dark-skinned, and very upbeat and positive.

"This school and these children are my life," she said. Her forthright and direct manner was punctuated by her strong voice.

"They bring me so much joy." A smile crinkled her eyes.

I saw great love in her warm, dark eyes and chuckling voice.

Never the quitter, I asked the principal a question.

"Do you know of anyone I could talk with to get an audience with the king? I brought him a present from the chief of the Cherokees. They live in my region in the US." My palms were together in a pleading gesture.

"Oh, my, no," she said. She took a step back, eyes wide. "It is nearly impossible. There are many steps you must go through to accomplish this. It is very time-consuming."

"Well, thank you anyway," I said, trying not to be disappointed.

It was worth a try.

"Now tell me about your challenges in this school," I said.

The principal took us to a preschool classroom. Children were working on vocabulary. They giggled as we entered.

"Our main problems," the principal said, "are resources, teacher training, and sign language." Her voice immediately brightened as she talked about her beloved school and children.

"Sign language is a very complicated issue at schools for the deaf." She leaned her head toward me.

"Most teachers don't know it. In KZN, we don't have any teacher training programs for elementary school teachers or for special education teachers." She stepped back, punctuating the statement by her movement and raised eyes.

"Amazing," I said.

"Also, the deaf children do not have access to a variety of story-books or textbooks to read."

How does anyone expect children to read if they don't have books?

As we walked into a room housing a dozen 7- and 8-year-olds, I glanced out the window across the space separating the building for deaf children from the building for hearing children. I saw a room in the opposite wing stacked with books.

"Have you thought of borrowing the books from across the way?" I said.

"Oh, no," she said. Her vowels were drawn out and low. Her voice held the same sense of disbelief as it had when I asked her about the king.

"Those are hearing books and not books for deaf children." The pitch of her voice went up.

What does that even mean? A book is a book is a book. It remains the same no matter whether the reader is black, white, Indian, female, or deaf.

"Ah, yes, I see," I said. But I didn't see.

"This reminds me of the history of schools for the deaf in the US," I said. "Segregation of deaf children from hearing children, and segregation of black deaf children from white deaf children used to be the norm." I noticed several of the little boys scuffling with one another, as little boys are wont to do.

"I have been to several schools over the past few days," I said. "My impression is that resources for schools in the Indian, Black, and Coloured communities are different from resources in White communities. Is that the case?" I said this in a matter-of-fact voice.

"Oh, yes," she said. "It is getting a little better since the end of Apartheid, but we still have so many needs." Her shoulders slumped slightly.

We walked in and out of rooms. The edges of the posters on the walls were discolored and peeling, as if there for many years. Children took their naps on the concrete floor with just a shirt or wrap for a pillow.

We finished our tour around lunchtime and were treated to samosas, pimento sandwiches on white bread, and juice.

"Thank you for the tour," I said to the principal. "And thank you for the lunch. I love samosas."

"Please come back," she said. "You are welcome to visit with us any time you are here." She grasped my hand between both of hers. She patted it.

"It is always a benefit for the children to meet people from other countries," she said.

If only we had that attitude in the US.

"You are a wonderfully creative principal," I said, "and you manage to squeeze the most education out of the fewest resources. On my next visit, I will take you up on your invitation. In the meantime, here is my email address."

I handed her my business card. "I would be honored to keep in touch with you."

I definitely want to discuss this school with the group.

I mentioned my musings to Nan as we drove to the next school. "I attempted to bring a couple suitcases full of materials and supplies to the schools on my trip," I said. "I could bring only one. It was just so expensive."

"Yes," said Nan.

"I would love to send resources to the school if I can find a way." My voice sounded more like a question than a statement.

I know lots of people who would open their hearts and bookshelves to these children.

"The challenge is one of politics," Nan said. "Most schools cannot pay the high taxes required to retrieve a package from the Customs office." She turned off the dirt road and onto a paved highway.

"So, it gets back to money, then," I said. "Humans have an odd relationship with money. We willingly give others our things, but we hold fast to our money. Somebody will give you the shirt off his back, but don't ask him for 50 cents."

"Yeees," she said. She drew out the vowel, softly acknowledging this human failing.

"It is more expensive to mail a box of books than to purchase them outright," she said. "But therein lies another problem. There are few resources available to purchase."

This is real challenge.

"If it's like this near the city," I said, "what is it like in the rural schools?" Nan's head tilted. Her eyebrows raised.

"Not good," she said.

We rode on in silence for a while.

Our final visit was to the VN Naik School, a large, public high school for the deaf in downtown Durban. The Naik School was predominately Indian with a fair mix of Black and Coloured students and a sprinkling of Whites.

"Pleasure to meet you," the principal said. His shoulders were squared, his head held high.

He toured us around the school. The visit was similar to the other schools.

"Some of our teachers are on their afternoon break," he said. "Please join us for refreshments."

As I entered the teacher's workroom, I spied the ever-present samosas, pimento cheese sandwiches, and juice.

The teachers echoed the same concerns as other teachers had.

"We need more resources for the students," said one. She pushed herself away from the table.

This sounded like a mantra she had spoken many times to no avail. I took notes on a pad of paper.

"Our teachers need ongoing training in sign language," said another, "and we need a decision on which sign language to use." She gestured toward the other teachers.

They murmured their agreements.

"Is there a language committee looking at that in the province," I said. "Which language should they all have to learn?" I was writing as fast as I could.

As I expected, there was disagreement among the teachers. Each of them championed the language closest to her heart.

"We need better trade school options for our older students," said another teacher. "We have such a high unemployment rate in the city. How are these students to find work if they have no usable skills?" The pitch of her voice raised as she stated her opinion.

"Yes," "quite right," and "such a tragedy waiting to happen," the other teachers said in return. "Our students are at a disadvantage to the rest of the world," said one more teacher. "They can use the internet at school, but they have no support for their studies at home. We can help the students who live in the dormitories but not the ones who go back home after school." Frustration in the room reached its peak, as if they had said this all before and expected no resolution.

The principal eyed the clock. He motioned for us to leave.

"The school bell is about to ring," he said, "and we need you to move your car or you may be caught in the line of vehicles." We walked weaving among the students.

He escorted us down the stairs, checking his watch frequently.

"Thank you," I said. We reached the exit near the parking lot.

"I will take your concerns back to my group. We are trying to determine where best we can focus our support. We appreciate your hospitality and look forward to working with you in the future."

Back in the car, I buckled the seatbelt, then turned to Nan. "Before coming to South Africa, I watched the movie, Soweto. It chronicled the protests against the use of Afrikaans in schools. I know Afrikaans was the language of the White Dutch immigrants."

"Yes," she said. Her voice remained calm.

"They came to South Africa in the 1700s and took over the gold and diamond mines," she said. "Afrikaans was a new language, separate from Dutch."

"The movie also showed the teachers using Afrikaans with the children. Were you in Durban at the time?" I asked. I hoped she would expand on my question.

"Yes, I was. In 1974, the Apartheid government established the Afrikaans Medium Decree. This required all tribal-speaking Black children to speak Afrikaans in school. Desmond Tutu called this, "the language of the oppressor.""

I've heard that before. I get it now.

"Many children were harshly treated for not learning Afrikaans. In 1976, tens of thousands of high school students in Soweto participated in an uprising. Fifteen-hundred white policemen re-sponded brutally, killing countless innocent school children."

And all due to intolerance of the heritage language of others.

"That must have been unbearable," I said. Sadness washed over me.

"It was and it still is for many." Her jaw tensed and slacked. "The memories are difficult to bear."

"You know," I said. "Mahatma Gandhi said, 'The true measure of any society can be found in how it treats its most vulnerable members.' By this measure, the Apartheid government fell exceed-ingly short."

"Yeees," she said, in that can I get an amen tone.

"About the teachers' comments this afternoon," I said, "Is the school situation still as bad as back then?"

"Not as bad as then but still bad. Our educational system is in great need of reform. There are still inequities."

We drove the last few blocks back to the B&B in silence, each lost in her thoughts. Across the schools, the teachers' concerns were forming a clear pattern.

"I need to share this with Sue, Gwen, and Hayward," I said. "My fact-finding mission has given me more to think about than I anticipated."

Chapter 7

Ixopo

Luck was mine. Several days of meetings, visits, and consultations passed. I was ready to do something other than to walk in and out of classrooms. Here was our chance. This day we were going to Ixopo, formerly Stuartstown.

We gathered at the picnic table.

"I still haven't mastered the X click in Ixopo," I said. "It's not for lack of trying."

"Neither have I," said Gwen. "I pronounce the X like a K, like ee-koe-poe." She grinned with her whole body, top teeth on her bottom lip and shoulders scrunched up.

"When I was a kid," she said, "I read *Cry, the Beloved Country*, by Alan Paton. Did you?"

"As a matter of fact, yes I did," I said. "when I was in high school."

"Well that was set in Ixopo," she said. "The Dutch named the town in 1878 after Mr. Stuart, the magistrate."

"Taxis are here," our hostess said. She poked her head through the doorway to the main house.

We said our goodbyes, weakly clicking Ixopo as we headed out the doors. Dewey stayed behind. He planned to play tourist for the day.

The taxis dropped us off at DUT, where we would board the university van to take us to our destination. Strini met us at the door.

"Come into the conference room," he said. "Be comfortable. We're leaving just now."

He motioned us to some seats around a conference table and hurried out the door. We waited patiently, chatting about much of nothing.

"This is your first trip out to the bush, right?" Gwen said to Hayward, Janice, and me.

"Yes, it is," I said. I chose a seat at the end of the conference table.

"I'm excited at the prospect," Hayward said. He leaned up against the door jamb, arms crossed.

"Me, too," said Janice. We smiled at one another.

"Let me tell you a bit about it, then," Gwen said. "The bush is a sparsely populated area of KwaZulu Natal, or KZN. Vegetation ranges from lush to sparse, depending on proximity to the mountains."

She strolled aimlessly around the conference room as she spoke. "And they pronounce the Z in KZN like the British do, K-Zed-N."

"Yes," I said. "I heard that as I was traveling around with Nan yesterday."

"In the 1990s, before the end of Apartheid," Gwen said, "there were a lot of armed conflicts in the region." She pointed the back of her right hand in our direction, circling it round and round to punctuate her words.

"You mean between the Afrikaners and the Zulus?" I said. I studied some of the history, but this was the extent of my knowledge.

"Yes," said Gwen. "Some of it. But, also between the African National Congress (ANC) and the Inkatha Freedom Party (IFP). The ANC is the largest political party in South Africa, the IFP the fourth." Her hand went back and forth, demonstrating the different sides of the conflict.

"Ask any of the residents here. They remember the conflicts vividly." Her hand dropped to her lap.

Death and destruction have left physical and emotional scars everywhere.

Lavern's administrative assistant, Lalitha, a lovely Indian woman, dressed in American-style clothing, joined us.

"Here you are," she said. Her soft and fluid voice had the gentleness of the other Indian women we had met.

"Please enjoy some refreshments." She set down a tray. It was laden with the ubiquitous samosas and fruit juices. She smiled with eyes wide open and walked out of the room.

"I wonder what the hold-up is," Sue said. "Any ideas?"

I admired her laid-back demeanor, almost yawning the question.

"No," said Gwen. Her 'no' sounded almost like a question.

"Not a clue," said Hayward. He moved from the wall to the chair and sat down, just in time to rise again as Lavern entered the room.

"Sincere apologies," said Lavern in his deep, cultured voice. "There is a teachers' strike outside campus, and we have not been able to secure transportation or clearance to leave safely." His voice was calm and slow. "We cannot use a campus vehicle, nor can we exit the front gate. We are sorting it out, though."

Sorting it out. Another common South African expression.

Sorting it out in this context, it turned out, meant recruiting personal cars. Nan, Strini, and Ela would drive us to our meeting.

After 10 or 15 minutes, Lavern reentered the room. He was as composed as ever. Back held straight. Head high.

"We have the necessary vehicles now and the back gate has been opened," he said. "Sue and Gwen will ride with Nan. Hayward and Janice will ride with Strini."

"Susan," he said to me. "Would you care to ride with Ela?"

Care to? Jackpot!

"That would be lovely. Thank you for the opportunity."

I realized I was swiveling around in the conference room chair.

Compose yourself, girl.

When all cars arrived, we got into our designated vehicles. Long lines of protestors were outside the campus fencing. There was loud and angry chanting.

I climbed into Ela's little blue car, and she drove us through the back gate and safely away from campus.

My palms were sweating, in part from the loud chanting and in part from the temperature, already warm for so early in the day.

"I have to admit, I felt a little uncomfortable back there. Not sure why. It was just a teachers' strike. I don't think safety was an issue."

"There is always a reason to be cautious about safety in South Africa," said Ela. "Most adults living today remember brutality at the hands of the police. Or they remember violent clashes within factions in the cities and rural townships." She scanned the traffic to make a turn off the side road and onto a larger street.

"Today we had the potential for a clash," she said, "and so we were mindful of your safety." Her demeanor was calm.

"Protests always hold the potential to escalate. One must be very careful in arranging protests because there are always elements who will try to usurp the energy for their own purposes. But there should be no conflict this time."

That's a relief.

Ela changed the subject. "Have you been enjoying your visit in Durban this week?" Her voice was soft and gentle with a slight, endearing waver.

"It has been so fascinating. I have a few more questions for you. Do you mind?"

"Not at all, I suspected you have some." She smiled knowingly. Corners of her mouth raised, lips closed. She had been through this before with countless visitors to her country.

"Yes, I do and feel free to stop me if I get annoying."

"I am happy to answer as best I can," said Ela.

Cars, trucks, and taxis were all around us.

"Nan and I took a tour of several schools for the deaf yesterday." My knees were wedged against the dashboard.

"The schools seemed still to be segregated, with Blacks primarily in one school and Indians primarily in another." I felt somewhat uncomfortable mentioning this.

Hmm. I need to unpack this feeling sometime. It shouldn't feel uneasy discussing discrimination.

"I saw a handful of white students integrated in some. Are most of the schools in SA still segregated?"

Ela drove on, forming her answer. Short in stature, she leaned forward over the steering wheel, back straight, grasping the wheel tightly. She looked intently at the road, chin jutting forward.

"Yes, it is an unfortunate story. I have lived through this my whole life. Growing up on the Settlement, I learned of Gandhiji's struggles in KZN." Her words flowed out as if she had told this story many times.

"Gandhiji, himself, was beaten and jailed while trying to resolve many of the inequities non-whites faced." She made no gestures, just stared at the road ahead.

"My father, in turn, was beaten and jailed as he continued to strive for racial equality. I was also arrested and then placed under house arrest."

Ho boy, I need to circle back to that one.

"You must have had such a sense of unease as a child," I said, "knowing this violence was going on all around you."

I pictured a little Ela, growing up in such difficult times. My heart felt compassion for her.

"I protested in my college days," I said, "but I never saw the kind of violence you did."

Your cultural privilege is showing again.

"The struggle is multi-generational," she said, "and it is world-wide. Martin Luther King studied Gandhiji's approach to peaceful conflict. You have seen it yourself in the United States. It is a continual cycle of improvements then problems then improvements. We must not be discouraged by the problems if we hope to continue to see improvements."

Significant advice to ponder. Such a juxtaposition. The lessons of protest in the US explained to me through the filter of a Gandhi. What a unique opportunity to expand my world view.

"We can speak more about this later," she said. "We are approaching our destination." She ducked her head and peered up at the sky.

"I hope the weather holds for us," she said. "You asked about the race groups the other day. You will see a different group here. Many are Zulu bushmen and women of the local tribes. But you will also meet Coloured people as well."

"I have been wondering about that," I said. We don't make that differentiation in the US." She seemed unruffled by my indecorous interruption.

"Coloured people are any of the mixed-race residents of the area. Some are Indian and Zulu, some are Afrikaner and Indian, any combination, really," she said. "But in Ixopo you will see many light-skinned, blue-eyed, non-white people. When Stuart settled in this region and brought several others with him, there was inter-marriage among the races."

A brief cloud burst came and went. Ela turned on the windshield wipers. We passed from under the cloud.

"Is there a pecking order to this?" I asked. "I mean, is one of the non-white races subject to prejudice more than the others?"

"Unfortunately, yes," said Ela. Her voice wavered a little. "White people are still privileged among the race groups. They are more present on the western side of the country."

The car began to slow.

"After White people, Indians hold higher positions, then the Coloured people, and then the Black races. The conflict is not only Whites against the non-Whites but among the non-White races as well. And across tribes." She spoke with quiet, yet assured authority born of experience.

Presently, the car pulled up to a small, brick building at a cross-roads. Several other buildings were located nearby. They seemed to have popped up out of nowhere after the long stretch of green croplands that changed to arid grasslands.

What struck me was the small cement block gas station next to the little municipal building. It had a sign posted on a side door that read, "Airtime."

Interesting. All the schools have limited resources, but everyone has a cell phone, and cell towers abound.

"I didn't see many buildings or houses along the way, only sparse settlements," I said. "And every so often, a cell tower would rise up to the sky. I noticed many of those little round houses, too. What are they called?"

"Those are the native rondavels," she said. "They are traditional dwellings with conical thatched roofs."

"Well, they are just so charming."

Charming? That was a stupid thing to say. I have no idea what they are for. This isn't a fairy tale.

I changed the subject. "Before our next meeting starts," I said, "would you tell me what you hope the outcome will be?" We unbuckled our seatbelts and waited for the other two cars to park.

"The purpose of this meeting in Ixopo is for your group to hear the challenges to improving human services, including education," she said. "We have been collaborating with Gwen and Sue for a while and hope to expand your university's involvement. I arranged this meeting so you could hear for yourself what the needs are."

"Thank you. That's what I thought, but I wanted to see if you have a personal agenda for the meeting." I opened the car door, finally stretching my legs.

"Other than exploring a collaboration," she said, "I would prefer to let the participants speak to your delegation for themselves. People are much more receptive to change if it is a change they have requested."

We entered the block and brick building on the corner of two very narrow roads. The entry room had a small table and chairs set randomly around the room. The inner room had a well-used meeting table with chairs spaced closely together around the table. A dozen local participants ranging in age from late 20s to 50s crowded with us around the table.

So many young ones. I feel old.

"Please allow me to introduce our delegation," said Ela. She named the five of us for the attendees.

The spokesman for the local group introduced his colleagues as well. Then he began his welcome speech.

"It is with great (he trilled his r) pleasure that we host your delegation today." He was dressed in a short-sleeved, plaid shirt and khaki pants. He spoke in a voice louder than I expected given the semi-formal situation and size of the room.

"Ours is a small but strong community dedicated to preserving its rich heritage while advancing the educational, cultural, health, and spiritual well-being of its citizens." He spoke slowly, emphasizing his words with expansive arm movements. His grammar was impeccable.

"We have experienced many trials and tribulations throughout our great history and, as a community, have overcome these, always with an eye to the future rather than to the past." He was standing, scanning systematically from participant to participant.

So dignified. So passionate. This is fascinating, more of an oratory than an opening statement. Similar to our first meeting with principals and teachers at DUT. Oratory is a lost art in the US. It's a treat to listen to.

As he spoke on, I glanced around the room, noticing the eclectic assembly of skin tones, eye colors, and form of dress from native to modern, casual to formal. The oration ended.

"Our guests would very much like to hear now from you, our hosts," said Ela, "regarding the challenges you are facing in this region." As always, her voice was soft and quiet. Her high pitch rose and fell in an inviting manner.

No further invitation was needed. Questions and concerns poured from the group. "Schools are doing their best here to educate the children," said one participant, also a local principal. "We are not able to support them all. We must have more facilities." He was in a suit jacket, sweat forming rings under his arms.

I could feel his anxiety.

"To come to school, children must wear uniforms. Families cannot always afford the uniforms. And we have nothing but used books. See here."

He showed me a textbook from the national repository that was well over ten years old.

"White schools get the modern textbooks," he said. "Our children get the cast-offs."

"Yeees," another participant said. She drew out the vowel sound in that low and slow honied tone I had come to appreciate.

"And the books are torn and marked," the next participant said. Her eyes screwed up in concern.

"This makes the children feel as if they are less important, not worthy of good books and materials." She spoke this in the broad, rounded vowel sounds of the local people.

"And we have no trade schools out here," said one of the high school teachers. "Without training in a trade, students are tempted to move to the cities, where there is worse poverty and crime."

He echoed the concern of the principal at the trade school Nan had taken me to.

"The answer cannot be for everyone to move to the cities," said Ela. "Who will tend the crops if everyone is in the cities? More trade schools need to be available in rural areas."

Such stirring words and such a serene demeanor. How does she do it?

"A rondavel would make the perfect option for small trade schools around the hills," she said. "Not everyone needs to sit in a modern-day school building."

There were nods. The murmurings within the room were becoming louder.

"Another problem we have," said a principal, "is poor access to the internet. The world is rushing past us quickly, and our children keep falling behind without adequate access." He tapped his fist lightly on the table.

"And many of them come from homes where the parents' generation did not even have the first year of schooling." His fist tapping grew in intensity, emphasizing his last four words.

"This creates a need for social programs to assist the parents in reading to their children. No parent wants to appear ignorant or foolish to his child."

The passion within the speakers' voices became more pronounced with each concern expressed. The meeting continued in this manner for 90 minutes.

"I see we are coming upon the lunch hour," our host said. "I hope we may continue this conversation as we are allowing our guests to refresh themselves."

He invited us to the adjacent room, where a table was laden with samosas, cheese sandwiches, fruit juices, and chicken satays. Chicken strips on skewers. Various cut-up vegetables were also on the menu. We took paper plates from the stack at the end of the table, then walked around choosing what we were inclined to eat.

We sat or stood around the table in smaller groups, each of us listening to the concerns of those in that group. I sat with Janice and three of the local women.

"I remember Ela said you are a nurse," one woman said to Janice. Her hair was wrapped in a brightly colored, tall turban.

"I am a nurse as well," said another woman. "But I am the only nurse for this entire region."

I could hear the exhaustion in her voice.

"I can train helpers to do visits for me to check on my patients," she said, "but I do not even have the basic equipment like stethoscopes to send with them. Diabetes is also a challenge."

"This is just appalling," said Janice. She patted the woman on the back of her hand.

"I can certainly find some boxes of stethoscopes for you."

She promised to find a way to get some stethoscopes out to the region.

I hope she has better luck with the stethoscopes than I did when I tried to get reading books into the country.

After lunch, we gathered again for a short period.

"I would like to invite some of you at this time to summarize the main topics we have discussed," said Ela. Her voice as sweet and calm as ever. "Not just the problems, but a key thought surrounding each problem that we may take back with us, each to his own place, to consider ways of addressing the need."

She orchestrated this summary masterfully, born of decades of experience organizing group action. Hayward volunteered to speak.

"We, too, face problems in the schools in Georgia. Resources are always a challenge. We have addressed these with a principal's leadership council among the schools." He turned to the principal who spoke first. "Do you have sufficient internet access to include several principals in your area in some internet discussions?" he said.

"Yes," said the principal. Curiosity was in his eyes. He placed his elbows on the table, clasped his hands, and leaned forward.

"Then I would like to offer to engage in some conversations with that group about establishing a leadership council to support one another in addressing your challenges." Murmurs of approval ran through the participants.

"And I would like to assist you," said Janice. She turned to the nurse.

"I am sure we can find some essential supplies for your assistants." More murmurings.

The nurse raised her hand to her heart, patting it in a gesture of thanks.

"We have been conducting workshops around Durban," said Gwen. "Sue, Susan, and I would be happy to do some teacher workshops around the region on our next trip."

Fantastic! There is going to be a next trip. I'm so lucky.

The meeting ended with pleasantries all around. We thanked our host and the participants for their hospitality and their openness to sharing their stories.

I got in the car with Ela to go to our next stop.

Wow. This is so eye-opening. I wish Ela would write her autobiography. Her take on Apartheid, racism, poverty, and action for change is just as important today as ever. I must talk with her about that.

We pulled away from the meeting building and drove on to our next appointment.

Chapter 8

Mr. Toad's Wild Ride

*H*ow in the world do I get myself into these crazy situations?

I was a 60-something, absent-minded professor on my first trip to South Africa. I am not brave. A friend calls me a loving hermit. Yet there I was, holding white-knuckled onto the passenger's seat of Ela's compact car, barreling up a tiny, winding road in Ixopo.

Ela, on the other hand, was a fearless little driver with nerves of steel. Flying down to the Southern hemisphere and all the way across a continent to the edge of the Indian Ocean did not compare to riding with this little demon behind the wheel. We careened past logging trucks on the wrong side of the mountain road according to my westernized nervous system. We approached the edge of a cliff. Its precipice was way too close for my comfort.

The beauty of the fields and mountains jerked me out of panic mode.

I remember Ela's comment that panic makes a situation worse. Guess I'll ask more questions to distract myself.

"Ela, when I was in your home, I noticed an unusual wooden spoon in your collection of treasures. I'm sort of a spoon collector myself." I shifted in my seat to face her better.

"I'm sure there is a story behind yours. Would you mind telling it to me?"

"Not at all," she said.

The car shook with every passing vehicle on the narrow two-lane road.

"I come from a long history of protesting against injustice," she said. "Not just Gandhiji, but also my parents. My father went to prison in 1953 for protesting against discrimination. When he came out, he told us about a gangster who was in prison with him."

"Oh my," I said. This was equally in response to her story as to the closeness we were tailing a logging truck.

"The gangster," she said, "was serving a huge sentence for murdering someone, but in prison he looked after my father. He made sure my father wasn't given a hard time. The guards would take all the prisoners outside in the hot sun, but my father wasn't well, and the gangster would tell the guards 'Just leave the man here.'"

I shook my head, clucking my tongue in disbelief at the story and the closeness of the precipice.

Just look away.

"The guards feared the gangster, even in prison," said Ela, "so they listened to him. He showed my father compassion even though he was a violent man. The gangster made a little spoon out of wood and gave it to my father. I still have that little spoon, the one you saw. You see, there is good in everybody and these stories teach you how to see the good in a person and not condemn people."

Yes, and you need to write these stories for others.

"It's easy for people to condemn others," I said. "To pigeon-hole them into the category of 'the other.' That leads to a lot of violence in the world. It makes peaceful, non-violent protest difficult as well." My knees were jammed against the dashboard.

"Yes," Ela said. "Non-violent protest can only be successful with lots of popular support. You can't have a non-violent struggle without doing the groundwork. When you look at Gandhiji's struggle, or my father's, or the civil rights movement in the United States, you had to go door-to-door to make the issue known."

We turned onto a narrow road that wound up the hillsides. "Is this a part of the process you went through when making non-violent protests?" I said. I shifted my knees from right to left, trying to uncramp them.

"Yes," she said. "Once we made the choice, we had to start building support. It was only when we had sufficient popular support that we could mount the campaign and go forward. If you move without that kind of support, you can't have a successful movement."

She looked in the rear-view mirror and edged even closer to the precipice to allow another car to whiz past.

"Yes," I said. "I can see that. It's probably why so many protests flare up but lose their energy fast."

This feels like Mr. Toad's Wild Ride. A favorite childhood story.

"Yes, you have to believe in the cause you are standing up for. You have to believe in your own power. Those two things are absolutely essential. If you have doubt about the cause, or the struggle within yourself, or your own ability, you are not going to be able to convince other people."

How does she do that? Remain so calm while speaking of conflict.

I was still eyeing the road. "But it's not so easy to convince other people to care about your own cause," I said.

"No," she said. "Not at all. There is a lot of fear involved."

I was grateful the road flattened out for a bit.

"First you have to build up confidence in the cause," Ela said, "and then you can start mobilizing the people. That takes a lot longer than just to go and get a gun and shoot the person, like the gangster who was with my father did. So, at the end of that violent conflict, he had more enemies and didn't solve the problem. If you take the time, you can transform people."

Although a sunny day, we rode into another rain shower.

"In my experience," I said, "most people want to win fast. They want to defeat the other guy and be done with it."

The road was becoming steeper again.

"It is not about defeating people and a winner or a loser, or a jailer or a prisoner," she said. "It's about transforming people and it's a much better way of dealing with conflict than to take the gun and go and shoot somebody."

I pondered this, elbow on the armrest, chin on my fist.

"So," I said, "you're saying there is good in everyone? Do you really believe that? What about someone who is a sociopath? What makes one person a Gandhi and another person a Bundy?"

I referred to the man who murdered 36 young women in the US in the 1970s. I was about the age of his victims at that time and the stories in the news unnerved me.

"It is how I have been taught," Ela said.

She didn't offer a distinct yes or no.

"And parents should share these stories with their children. That is how they learn about human nature. They do not learn about true human nature from fairy tales, where bad people are bad and good people are good. There isn't always a happy ending. Likewise, people are not always as they seem on the surface."

The rainstorm passed.

"What kinds of stories would you tell children," I said.

I hadn't checked the closeness of the wheel to the edge of the road for a while. Either the distraction was working, or the road was widening.

"My mother told me a story about a woman who used to work with my aunt in India," Ela said. "She was a doctor, and one day a thug in the village came with his gang, kidnapped her and took her to his home. To her surprise the kidnapper's wife was going to have a baby and she was in difficulty, and so she helped to deliver the baby safely. After all that, they brought her back and left her in the ashram and from that time forward, if anything happened, they would be there to help the ashram, showing their compassionate side."

"That's a beautiful story," I said.

Another one she should write.

"Gandhiji use to say, 'Hate the sin; love the sinner.' We have to show compassion," she said. "We have to know why someone has come to do evil things if we want to help that person or to move past their evil deeds."

A truck passed us heading the other direction. Strong, young workers, all males, dirty from the sugar cane fields, were crowded close together on the truck's flatbed.

"That's hard for most people," I said. "To look past evil or even to look past inconvenience and to see the other guy's perspective. Does the degree of evil have a role? I mean, when someone cuts me off while I'm driving, it's easier to excuse them than when they try to hurt someone I care about."

I hope I'm not missing the point.

"Well," said Ela. "Let's look at that."

The truck we were behind pulled off the road onto a dirt path leading to a small outcropping of structures. Ela sped up.

"There was a lot of the violence going on during Apartheid," Ela said. "This was being perpetrated not only by the oppressed people but by former members of the Special Branches of law enforcement, both colours. It did not seem to make a difference. All of them sought retribution."

"And retribution only makes matters worse," I said. "Your grandfather said it very well, 'An eye for an eye makes the whole world blind.'"

What am I doing, quoting Gandhi to a Gandhi?

"Yes," said Ela. "When I was working as a social worker, I had a complaint from a woman whose husband was abusing her violently. He happened to be with the Defense Force. He came to my office for a meeting during which he cried and told me a horrifying story. It was quite confidential at the time. He told me that the Defense Force would take soldiers and police they felt were brave and could tolerate atrocities to the Karoo."

"Where is that?" I asked.

"The Karoo is a sparsely populated, semi-desert area near Capetown. The Cango Caves are there. Today they are tourist attractions, but back then, one part of the caves was for tourists and another was where the army took people to brainwash them. I don't know what methods they used, perhaps shocks."

How does she remain so serene, talking about such violence? I need to practice this myself.

"Their purpose firstly was to ingrain absolute obedience into the men so they would absolutely do whatever they were told," she said. "He told me he could take his fingers and remove someone's eyeballs. That's how he was."

Goose bumps ran up and down my back. "Oh, my God." I said. "That's awful. I would have been terrified of him. What did you do?"

"I listened quietly," Ela said. "I composed myself. He was giving a confession and it was not my place to judge him. He told me he could not readjust now that he was home. He feared that if he became angry, he could not control his temper. He feared he could pull out his wife's or someone else's eyes. They were taught to be brutal. How much of it is the truth, I don't know, but that's what he said. They were trained in Nazi-like brutal methods of torture and death. Terrible things were done to members of the Defense Force and in turn, terrible things were done by the Defense Force." She spoke so calmly of this.

I sat, stunned for a moment. More goosebumps were navigating around my skin.

Perhaps her calmness comes from living with this knowledge for so many decades. Perhaps acceptance is just part of the Gandhi nature.

"That's tragic," I said. "There's a popular saying in the US, 'hurt people hurt people', meaning that someone can enact all manner of disrespect, bullying, abuse, and torture against another if that same disrespect, bullying, abuse, and torture happened to them. We all have the potential for good, for love, for compassion and we all have the potential for evil, for hate, and for coldness."

I found it difficult to make sense of this horror while surrounded with the exquisite, verdant landscape. Azure sky, picturesque hills of stately sugar cane, and deep, lush valleys were all around.

"Yes," she said. "And it is up to the parents to be a model for love and compassion, and to speak out against bullying, abuse, and disrespect."

We drove on. "Ela you know, you really should write your auto-biography." I couldn't shake the thought.

Again, she said, "I would not know where to start."

"I would be happy to help you. If I could audio-record some of our conversations and have them typed up, all you would need to do is reorganize them as you saw fit and you would have a book. It would be beneficial to many people."

Her mouth smiled but her eyes did not.

A logging truck whizzed past, shaking the little car, reminding me I was on the precipice of a cliff. I changed the subject, ready for a lighter topic.

"Apropos of nothing," I said. "Is there a way for us to meet the Zulu king?" Her grip on the wheel remained as tight but her eyebrows raised.

"For what purpose?" she asked.

I told her the story of the basket and how I would like to complete my mission and deliver it to him. As did everyone else, she explained how difficult it would be to accomplish.

"Well, then," I said, "Do you think Strini or Lavern could deliver it to him?" She did not comment right away but craned her neck to look ahead.

"Perhaps," she said.

Somehow, we safely reached our destination off the logging path, along a deeply rutted dirt road. We drove up an equally rutted incline, which was the entrance to the Hluthankunga (hloo-tan-koon-ga) Primary School. Sue and Gwen had already arrived with Nan. Janice and Hayward were back in Durban with Strini.

Prying my now pretzel-shaped body from the front seat, I ran up the incline to catch up with Ela. Her soft voice and diminutive frame hid the fact that she has the physical and mental constitution of a lioness.

Disheveled, somewhat dizzy, and out of breath, I reached the group just in time to shake the hand of Mrs. Norris, principal of the school. Her creamy coffee-colored face set off striking blue eyes.

"Welcome, welcome to our little school," Mrs. Norris said. "We are so pleased you have taken your time to visit us. The children have a surprise for you." Her voice was motherly, her actions quick.

Clearly a multi-tasker. She's the quintessential elementary school principal.

We walked across the dirt and tufted-grass parking lot and around a tree at the corner of the school. The schoolyard sat on a knoll overlooking the most spectacular collection of greens and blues, hills and skies.

I saw the school office building over Ela's head. Suddenly, voices from half a dozen classrooms around the schoolyard sang out, "Home, home on the range. Where the deer and the antelope play." The timing was off, the rhythm was off, but the voices were pure and sweet.

I haven't thought of that song in decades.

"The children wanted to surprise you with some traditional American music," said Mrs. Norris. "They are so proud you are visiting us."

"That's so sweet of them," said Gwen.

"I love it," said Sue.

"They sound wonderful," I added.

We shared knowing glances, tickled by the choice of a song we had not heard since our own childhoods.

We toured the school, going from room to room, each in its own separate wooden or cement block house, kindergarten through grade five. In one classroom, the children sang for us again.

"Your singing is so lovely," we said. "Thank you for making us feel so welcomed."

In another classroom, students were practicing their oratory skills. One young lady stood up, struck a powerful stance, raised her little fist in front of her, waist high, and began her oration.

"That's the cutest thing I've ever seen," I said to Sue and Gwen when we left the room. "She was all fire and brimstone."

"You don't ever see children in our schools learning to stand and deliver with that level of confidence," said Sue.

"When did we stop preparing students to take a stand like that and defend it," I said. "I don't ever recall learning that as a child. It would have done me wonders."

They nodded in agreement.

Wait, yes it would have done me wonders or yes, the schools should do it?

Our tour ended right around afternoon break time and we were treated to the ever-present samosas and fruit juice. While eating, we conversed with the teachers, most of them Coloured, with their mixed skin-tones and their light brown or blue eyes.

The teachers expressed similar concerns as those we heard earlier in the day. "We do not have modern textbooks," said a blue-eyed Coloured woman.

"We do not have enough reading materials," said another. She wore a smock over her dress in the design of the South African flag.

"Many of our children live with their grandparents, who never went to school," said another. "We need to help them become literate enough to help their children with schoolwork." She was the oldest among the group.

"And we do not have enough space to accept all the children. Too many of them have no education at all," said the last. Her shoulders slumped as she said this, much like I saw from those who shared their concerns in other schools. The pattern was clear now.

The school day ended, and we still had a ride back to Durban. Mrs. Norris walked with us to our cars after the break.

"Thank you for your kind visit. It will be a topic of conversation among the children for weeks," she said.

"We thank you as well," said Gwen. "Please know that we are going to brainstorm ways to address some of your needs. Tackling your literacy challenge is definitely within our skill set. We'll keep in touch with you and are already making plans to return next year."

Looks like we'll be writing some grant proposals when we return home. I hope the ride down the mountain isn't as intimidating as the ride up.

Chapter 9

A Trip Back in Time

Riding back to Durban, a million questions ran through my head.

"I am sure you have more questions for me," Ela said. "You may ask them." She smiled, her lips closed.

You don't have to ask me twice.

"I would love to hear more about your early years on the Settlement, and about Apartheid, and I have quite a few questions from our visit today."

I hope I'm not overwhelming her with my insatiable curiosity. I don't want to be pushy, but she's so fascinating to me.

"Well," she said. "Let's start with the Settlement. We all had tasks we were assigned to do, even the little ones. We had water in a borehole, but it was totally undrinkable as it was very saline. We washed clothes and dishes with it. Drinking water was obtained from a tank, which was filled with rainwater harvested from our roof. But when we did not have enough rain, then we had to struggle to get drinking water."

She always perked up when talking of her childhood on the Settlement. Voice chipper. Speech quickened.

"We used to go to a little canal on the large sugar estate in our neighborhood. They used this to irrigate the plantation. It had lovely clear water. We would carry it home. And then my mother would boil it, strain it through a muslin cloth, and keep it for drinking in a clay pot."

We are so spoiled today. Such effort, just for a drink of water.

"I have never tasted that kind of water since my childhood. It was so refreshing in the hot weather when we had a severe shortage of water. It was a long walk with the bucket. Not a very big bucket because I was trying to balance it on my head. It was an experience I will never forget."

And all I have ever had to do was turn on the tap. We are only 10 years apart in age, but our experiences are from different eras.

"Often, I would be drenched, bringing home half to three quarters of a bucket of water. Of course, I did not have to do that daily. There were others, like my brother who is six years older than me, who would bring large quantities of water."

Pictures of little Ela balancing her bucket, the contents of which soaked her dress, crowded into my mind's eye.

"We also had to clean our toilets daily. We had a box of sand that had to be filled daily and the buckets emptied in a pit. Next, we threw sand over the contents in the pit so that no flies were attracted. Then we would clean and wash the toilet. After using the toilet, the sand in the box would be used to cover up the feces."

I have never before considered the challenge of keeping a latrine sanitary. As a child I had friends who had no indoor plumbing. Rather, they used an outhouse. No little blue pellets in the toilet tank for sanitation. No squirt bottles of chemicals. Glad I live with modern conveniences.

"A very important lesson for me," said Ela, "was that there was dignity in doing work no matter how mundane the work may be. But my parents did not ask us to do anything they did not do themselves. They cleaned the toilets as well. Gandhiji carried out all these tasks himself. It was ingrained in us, part of our heritage. And this is an important part of the tradition of servitude. If I feel a sense of repugnance for any work, then the answer is not to ask someone else to do it but to school myself to do it myself. This is because there is dignity in work, no matter how mundane or repugnant."

A third principle. There is dignity in work. This should be in every school curriculum.

"Those were some of the daily responsibilities we had to learn to do," Ela said, "in order to keep the place clean and not attract flies. These kinds of tasks required discipline, determination, precision, and economy of effort."

These stories flow from her, not at all a distraction to her driving. Good thing, given the narrow roads. Fortunately, there were fewer log trucks heading down the mountain this time of day.

"I can see that it was a very disciplined, purposeful, and principled life." I shifted my knees left and right more frequently than earlier in the day.

"Yes, 'Twas an important set of principles—discipline, precision of thought and action, and economy of effort."

Part of the Gandhi archetype and a fourth set of principles?

"What about determination?" I asked.

"I guess I developed that fairly quickly." Ela laughed, her head tipping back slightly. "I staged my first protest when I was nine years of age. This was a protest against my parents, so it was a hard-fought battle." She laughed, the corners of her eyes crinkling.

"Well, you learned from the best," I said.

"Indeed, my father and grandfather were involved politically in the struggle against Apartheid. My grandmother, Kasturba Gandhi, was just as much involved in the struggle as Gandhiji was. He acknowledged that she was the backbone of the struggle. So, growing up in that background of activism, I can't specify a moment when I became conscious of it. It grew and I grew into those principles."

"Same as your grandfather," I said. "His awareness grew through events in his life."

"Yes, in fact, Gandhi returned to India about 30 years prior to my birth, and on the occasion of the 100th anniversary of his return, President Nelson Mandela in a speech in India stated: "You gave us Mohandas; we returned him to you as Mahatma." But there was a

Mohandas and Kasturba Gandhi, Ela's Grandparents

time, when my parents felt I should be educated at home by them and I shouldn't go to the segregated schools that were present at that time. My father in particular objected. He didn't like the system of education under Apartheid. This is because it taught you from the point of view of the oppressors, of people who believed in Apartheid. To him it was like brainwashing."

We were getting closer to Durban. The landscape was leveling out. The roads were widening. The traffic was getting thicker.

"My father said, 'Why do you have to go to school to learn these lessons which are not true—you can learn at home!'"

"But like a little kid who wanted to follow other children in the neighborhood I protested. I said, 'No, I have to go to school' and so that was my first protest and I succeeded."

Is that a giggle I hear?

"It's always nice to win victories," she said, "because they help you find your own voice."

The hum of the road matched the soothing sound of her voice.

"This is necessary in the world today, to learn to ask for things that are achievable, and then ask for the next thing," she said.

So interesting. The organized side of my brain interrupted me. A fifth principle.

"How do you decide what is achievable?" I asked.

"You focus on what is achievable in the immediate future. When people start with the war and lose the first battle, they become despondent and lose faith in themselves and the struggle. Small victories are important. Going to public school was a small victory. It may not even have been a victory. I don't know, I might have learned better at home, but the point is, it was a victory. And this empowered me to continue to seek more victories."

"So, you think we should be teaching children at an early age to learn how to stand up for themselves and to take on challenge?"

I thought of the fire and passion in the voice and fist of the little orator we heard at the end of our school visit.

"Yes, children need help to learn how to fight for their rights, to ask for things that are reasonable, to organize well and to aim for the first little victory and then the next. This gives strength to continue. These influences were all around me. My parents were steeped in work for the community. Phoenix Settlement was a hub of activity. My parents spent time with people who came to seek their help. I remember when a neighbor, Reverend Shembe, had his July festival and housed hundreds of visitors in his settlement. He would come to my dad to seek permission to use the water from the well and the little stream on the Settlement property. When families living on land adjacent to the Settlement were evicted because the government wanted that land, they approached my Mum for temporary shelter. My parents willingly came to their rescue."

The air from the hills wove itself in and out of the windows. It was fresh and clean, a departure from the smell of the Indian Ocean.

"There was so much beautiful vegetation in Ixopo," I said. "Did you have farmland around the Settlement?"

"Yes, on the Settlement, everyone learned how to compost, plant, till, tend, and harvest vegetable and flower beds in an organic, ecological manner. There was joy in seeing the plants shoot out of the soil—eggplants, beans, peas, and fruit such as pineapples and mangoes, growing and ripening. This was indescribable. This joy remains with me to this day. But I admit to one failure of life on the Settlement. To this day I am afraid of things that crawl, from the smallest little worm in a bean pod to the reptile."

"Well that's an irony not to be missed," I said. "Overcoming your fear amongst the crush of souls in a jail van and living through the atrocities of Apartheid, and yet you are afraid of worms? I find that both amusing and comforting."

"I did learn that human beings should be caring not only towards other human beings but towards animals and towards nature and the environment as well."

"Ah," I said. Another principle? A sixth principle learned growing up Gandhi.

"Yes," she said. "To care about all living things, human and animal, and to be good stewards of Mother Earth. I learned this by age seven and during Partition, which was a particularly nasty time in the history of India. But I still don't like the crawly things. Sometimes it is not easy living a principled life."

Chapter 10

The Zulu King

The next morning, coffee mugs in hand, the GSU group talked about ways we might help the schools with the list of concerns they identified. More workshops? Materials? Preparing grant proposals? All of these were possibilities within our combined skill set. Still, there was no resolution to my basket problem.

"Gwen, I am beginning to despair of ever finding a way to get my basket to the King. Dr. Gawe seems to think it is improbable. I talked with Ela yesterday. I hoped she might have a personal contact with His Majesty. But she seemed to think it wasn't possible, either. I don't know what to do." My shoulders slumped.

What if I built this whole basket thing up in my head? What if I have to take it all the way back to the Chief?

"I'm sorry. I don't have any other suggestions for you," she said. She was standing beside the table. Her open eyes and placid smile showed compassion.

"I know he was Chancellor of the university at one point," she said. "Maybe we should talk with Lavern or Strini again."

"Good idea. Thanks." I was losing the little bit of hope I had with each passing minute.

From inside the main house, we heard our hostess's phone ring. Then a muffled voice. Then footsteps heading our way. Gwen turned toward the doorway just as our hostess arrived.

"Gwen, it's for you," she said. She beckoned Gwen inside with a gentle wave of her hand. Gwen walked into the house and disappeared around the corner.

"I wonder who that is," Sue said. She turned away from the doorway and looked at all of us.

"I hope they aren't having more problems because of the teacher's strike," she said.

What next.

"Here comes Gwen," she said. "I hope it's not bad news."

Gwen came back over to the table and sat down. Her face had a look of incredulity. Jaw slack, eyes wide, she turned to me.

"You must be living right," she said. She shook her head slowly.

"That was Lavern. He says the King is going to be at Queen Thandi's palace in the Midlands and you are invited to give him the basket there."

Dewey laughed his raucous laugh, upper torso thrust forward.

"Are you kidding me?" I jumped to my feet.

"No, I'm not," she said. Her smile of compassion turned to one of wonder.

"So," Janice said, "who is Thandi?"

"Thandi is one of the King's six wives," she said. "You need to get ready because a driver is on his way."

We looked around at one another, eyes wide, mouths open in disbelief and excitement.

"He can take four of you," Gwen said. "Sue and I have an appointment with one of the town's administrators."

She looked at me. "That leaves you, Dewey, Hayward, and Janice." She looked at Hayward and Janice.

"Two more spaces," she said. "Are you game to go?" She had a grin on her face. It was obviously a rhetorical question.

"Of course," they said. "We wouldn't miss this opportunity for the world."

Truth be told, because it seemed so unlikely this would happen, I had not given a second thought to what I would say to His Majesty.

But now we were going to the Queen's palace. In my mind's eye, it would be an informal get together, much as my visit to Principal Chief Hicks was, when I received the basket.

"Oh, my gosh," I said to Hayward. "What in the world am I going to say to him?" I nibbled the cuticle of my index finger.

I looked up into his face, searching for suggestions. Hayward is a distinguished gentleman and a polished speaker.

"Give me some ideas." I began to pace.

He placed a hand firmly on my shoulder. "I think you will do fine," he said. "Just speak from your heart."

My nerves kicked into high gear as we traveled out to the Midlands. It is a region northwest of Durban, characterized by lush, green, rolling hills and located near the Drakensberg mountain range.

We were on our way to meet King Goodwill Zwelethini ka BhekuZulu, ninth in a long line of rulers dating back to the 1700s. The most famous of these was Shaka, who united all the tribes under one rule.

Kay-bek-uh, kah-bek-oo? I'll just call him 'Your Majesty.' Scenes from the Tarzan movies of my childhood played in my head, warriors scantily clad in skins and feathers, spears in hand. I could hear the clicking of the movie camera from the back of the theater.

Rather than arriving at a private residence, we found ourselves at the Midlands campus of DUT. "I wonder if he had a change of mind?" I said to the group. "Maybe he has an office on campus and we're meeting with him there."

The campus was over-run with cars. People walked here and there.

Not many students, though, so perhaps this is a faculty function.

Our driver took us to a large masonry building, long with tall, wide windows running down both sides from one end to the other. He bade us exit the car.

"I will remain with the car until they inform me to pick you up," he said. "Do not worry. I will not leave without you." He tilted his head and bowed slightly from the waist.

An official-looking young man, possibly in his late 30s to early 40s approached us. He was dressed in a dark suit and starched white dress shirt. His rather uncomfortable looking tie was tight around his neck.

"Hallo," he said. "Are you the party from Durban?" He spread his hands open in a gesture of invitation.

"Yes," we said.

"Which one of you is Professor Easterbrooks?" I stepped forward and extended my hand. We made introductions all around.

"Please call me Susan," I said. He continued to call me by formal address.

"I am a representative of the King's advance organizing committee. His Majesty is here to launch a joint venture between Zulu farmers and the Chinese government." He spoke in impeccable British English with African overtones.

"The purpose of this venture is to provide support and training to the local women who will raise and grow exotic mushrooms."

Wait, what? Mushrooms? Am I Alice? Did I fall through the looking glass?

"These," he said, "will be sold both locally and internationally. This is one of China's many joint ventures across the country and the continent as a whole."

I thought we were going for a brief, informal visit with the King. Oh gee, we are last-minute intruders, crashing an international event.

"Please tell me," the representative said, "Is this your first audience with the King?" We were standing outside the event building. The mid-afternoon heat was noticeable. He never broke a sweat.

"Yes," we said.

We are like babes in the wood.

Everything seemed unique from the venue to the topography to the mounds of mushrooms. We saw them through the windows, displayed in large cases.

"Permit me, then, to provide you with some words about protocol." He folded his hands across his back as if in parade rest formation.

"You will be seated at one of the tables of dignitaries near the King's dais," he said. "You are permitted to talk with anyone except those on the dais, and you must never approach the King."

No problem there. All these serious-looking, muscular guys. Most likely bodyguards. Eyes darting everywhere. Clearly, I wouldn't make it past the first step in the King's direction, even if I tried.

"The master of ceremonies will open the event," said the King's representative. "There will be welcoming speeches from both delegations, a short program about the launch, and then respects will be paid." He turned to face me.

"Professor," he said. "When it is your turn to pay your respects, you will walk up to the dais and hand your gift to the gentleman at the podium. You will not give the King the gift. It must first be examined."

Well that's a first. Nobody has ever suspected me of being a terrorist before.

"Then you will make your speech."

My speech? I don't have a speech. I think I'm in shock. Steady, girl.

I nodded my agreement wholeheartedly.

"After all dignitaries have paid their respects, a luncheon will be provided. The King's tasters will go first, followed by the King and Queen."

Yikes. He has taster. There's a story somewhere, I am sure.

"Then the members of the Chinese and South African delegations will get their food, followed by those at the dignitaries' tables," the representative said. "Finally, the general audience will go through the line for their food." His stance never wavered. At parade rest. Calm yet authoritative. Warm yet official.

"After the luncheon, some of the local Zulu women will entertain you with customary songs and dances. The event will end with a speech from the King."

We saw several young dance troupes in our travels: at the restaurant, along the boardwalk, and then the children dancing for us at the school. This promised to be different as the dancers were local women, farmers, and community members.

"Once the program starts," the King's representative said, "you must remain in your seats. When the King signals the end of the event, you will have time to walk around and view the mushrooms. We will then proceed to the Mushroom Research and Training Centre, where His Majesty will unveil the plaque and launch the project. At the end of this stage of the event, your driver will be called, and he will meet you back in this location. Do you have any questions?"

Other than what in the world am I doing here?

"No, sir," I said. "You have explained this very clearly. Thank you."

He led us inside the event building. It was large and airy, with high walls and industrial lighting. The tall windows were surrounded by yellow walls. He escorted us to a table about 12 feet from the King's dais. Janice and Hayward sat with us as did a few members of the Zulu nation's administration. Also seated at the table was a serious, quiet gentlemen, perhaps one of the King's muscular guards. Perhaps not. He said very little the whole time.

The event began. It proceeded exactly as the King's representative described. A master of ceremonies began the event. In turn, each of the officials on the dais gave a speech about the importance of international relations and the high expectations for the mushroom endeavor. Speeches were in English with heavy Chinese or Zulu accents. Next, several from the dignitaries' tables below the King's raised dais went up to the podium, handed their gifts to the bodyguard, gave a short speech, and nodded to the King.

Now it was my turn. How I made it up to the podium without fainting, I will never know. What I said during my short speech, I do not remember. But there I was, on the dais with His Majesty in front of an international audience of several hundred people, staring out at tables of mushrooms, and thanking him for his indulgence.

"I share salutations from the Principal Chief of the Eastern Band of the Cherokees in the United States," I probably said. "He sends his warm greetings and honors you with this basket made by a member of his nation."

I handed the basket to the man behind the podium. My hands were shaking. The afternoon sun was coming in from the opposite windows, and I couldn't see my table, my colleagues, my husband. Mine was the only speech not related to the mushroom launch. This drew raised eyebrows from several in the Chinese delegation.

To my surprise, at the end of my speech, the King rose, approached me, and offered his hand.

Yes, I shook the hand of the Zulu King. A very firm handshake from a wide hand, his skin rough. My mind went blank.

He smiled. I returned to my table. To this day I marvel at the experience.

After the speeches, the assembly proceeded down the buffet table past a long line of full-sized, stainless steel chafing dishes. The King's tasters went first, then the King and Queen with the rest following.

At least 15 different items tempted us. Many of the dishes were made from exotic mushrooms—mushroom fritters, mushroom chutney, mushrooms in sauce, mushrooms on bread crust.

Feels like the shrimp scene from the Forrest Gump movie. "Shrimp creole. Shrimp kabobs. Fried shrimp. Lemon shrimp."

My husband's plate was loaded with beans, a tomato, rice, a boiled purple potato, chopped beets on greens, chicken, mushroom chutney, and a crispy mushroom fritter.

After the luncheon, a troupe of Zulu women danced and sang for us. They wore calf-length skirts, tops, drapes over the tops, and orange scarves over their shoulders. Their heads were adorned with the traditional Zulu hat, an isicholo (is-ee-ko-lo), woven and beaded. Their substantial garments were in considerable contrast to the skimpy costumes of the young troupe we saw on the boardwalk.

Local Dancers

The King gave his speech, the first part in English, the last in Zulu. Toward the end, he required all the men in the room to stand and follow him in a chant. He forbade the women to join. Dewey and Hayward did their best to mimic the final words and gestures with all the men.

"Do you know what you were saying?" the quiet gentleman at the table said. His voice was very deep, and it resonated through the air. He spoke slowly.

"You were pledging your fealty to the King," he said. "The final chant, in which you raised and lowered your fisted hand, was 'You are from elephant,' the hand gesture representing the elephant's trunk. Elephant is considered the strongest animal in our land. You honor the King by this gesture, and you have now sworn to defend our nation if required."

Dewey's shotgun blast laugh pierced the room, garnering stares from several of those around us. Hayward's eyes widened. He turned to look at Janice. She returned an amused smile.

"You are dismissed," said His Majesty.

Almost instantly, all those seated at the tables stood, forming a line to tour display after display of exotic mushrooms. They were exquisite, in colors and shapes I had never seen before. Pale yellows, light corals, grays, and every shade on the beige to brown spectrum imaginable.

"Look, Dewey," I said. "This one looks like a piece of a coral reef."

"And this one looks like a spiral rocket ship," he said.

"Please tell me these aren't little elephant's ears," said Janice.

We followed the mass of people to the research center. More speeches were given. The King pulled the cord to reveal the plaque behind the drapes. Applause erupted.

There was general milling around and I was starting to feel even more like an interloper among these people who were joyfully celebrating this historic joint venture.

Fortunately, the King's representative located us.

"Your driver is on his way," he said. "Do you remember the location where you are to meet him?"

"Yes, thank you," we all answered.

Mushrooms

"I will leave you at the restrooms to refresh yourselves for the return trip."

We thanked him again.

"Pleasure," he said. He nodded sharply, head tilted to one side, then moved on to his next obligation.

We proceeded to the men's and women's rooms to freshen ourselves for the trip back to Durban as instructed. I passed a woman as she was exiting the restroom. It had only one stall. Then it hit me.

Oh my gosh. That was Queen Thandi. I missed the opportunity to sit where Queen Elizabeth sat at our first restaurant, but I get to sit on a Queen's throne after all.

Chapter 11

Southeastern to Northwestern Hemisphere

The morning was fresh and sunny. But we felt low, as if someone turned down the dimmer switch on our spirits. This was our final day of 10 glorious days in Durban in April of 2010. We gathered around the picnic table one last time. None of us wanted to leave our newfound home and friends. All of us took to heart the struggles in this beautiful, complex land.

"Everyone has been so gracious," said Sue. "Wherever we went from the schools, colleges, and agencies to personal homes and events, everyone was so accepting." Her voice had a little catch in it.

"I agree," said Gwen. "Our presentations and consultations were well-received." She gave Sue a little squeeze around the shoulders.

"I, for one, am enthusiastic about our potential to affect positive change in some areas," said Hayward. His back was straight and strong, but his eyes were lowered.

"I'm sad to be leaving," I said. "But I am excited to go home. I miss my son."

The group opted for one final breakfast together at the same hotel where we started our adventure. Dr. Gawe, Lavern, Strini, and of course Ela joined the six of us.

This time the restaurant was filled with patrons. Happy chatter came from all directions. Dishes rattled as bus boys went about their business.

We went through the buffet line to fill our plates. The smells from the international fare commingled, creating a unique aroma, spicy yet sweet, ripe yet tangy. At the table, conversations started up again in the easy manner of friends who have shared many experiences.

"Strini, I forgot to take my big, green suitcase of books to the KwaVuLindlebe school when Nan and I visited. If I leave it with you, will you give it to Nan and ask her to deliver it for me?"

"Pleasure," he said. His fork and knife clinked on the plate. He ate enthusiastically. "I love a good breakfast."

"Lavern," I said. "Would you please thank Lalitha for me for all her kindnesses? She took care of all the little details for us, from feeding us to finding us pens when ours ran out of ink. She's a gem."

"True. And yes, it would be my pleasure," he said in that low, rich tone of his. It fit perfectly with his personal and professional stature.

We were all trying to squeeze the most out of our last visit. I kept peppering Ela with questions through breakfast, past coffee, and well after the table was cleared. "Ela, several things have stuck with me over the past few days. I am hoping you can give me a little more insight."

We sat across the table from one another. "I'll try." She set her tea down and listened intently. Her eyes never left my face.

"At the Settlement, our guide spoke of your grandfather's religious philosophy," I said. "I read that Gandhi studied with the Theosophical Society. I mentioned this to you because many of his sayings are consistent with that perspective. I know he was an avid student of religion. What was his religious perspective?" I sat back in my chair, ready to listen as intently as she had.

"Gandhiji's religion and philosophy of change were integrally intertwined," she said. "He thought there was a need for people to learn discipline in their religious practices and also in how they enacted change. Just protesting was not enough. He felt he needed to teach people what it meant to protest, how we should conduct ourselves and so on, and he saw the need for unity." A noisy group of patrons at the table beside us got up to leave. After they passed, she continued.

"This is why he developed his principles of spirituality," she said, "which are different from Hindu religion. Books were important, but religion taught you how to live a principled life and a belief in God. He didn't believe in religion as being rituals, as being confined to a church or a mosque or a temple. Religion must become a part of your life."

"It has to become who you are," I said.

"Yes, you must carry those spiritual principles into your life and your activism. That is what he taught the people in his ashram." She leaned forward and took a sip of tea. Chai tea, spicy, aromatic, and sweet-smelling.

"Are you talking about the Phoenix Settlement or about his ashram in India?" I said.

"Both. All different religious faiths, they all came and prayed together. They prayed outside, not in a building, and they were quite comfortable in praying in all the different faiths. They discussed questions of truth, honesty, values, integrity, compassion, love, love of the environment, of conservation, identification with the poorest of the poor as well as courage and fearlessness. As a child growing up, we used to recite his principles every day on the Phoenix Settlement."

So that is why her conversations yield so many principles. They are ingrained into the fabric of her life.

"One person who contributed to the understanding of Gandhiji's philosophy, was Martin Luther King. When you read Martin Luther King's work and you see how he describes Gandhiji's philosophy, you begin to understand it more, with greater clarity, because he puts it in clear language. King came to India to study about my grandfather. I included a section about him in the book I wrote about Gandhiji, called *Essential Values of Mahatma Gandhi.*"

Another example of how the principles filter into all her conversations. That makes so much sense now.

"But Ela," I said. "It's one thing to have people recite a set of principles and another thing to make a permanent change in human nature. Personal responsibility has to fit in there some-where, doesn't it?" My coffee was gone but I didn't need a refill. I was jazzed up enough by the conversation.

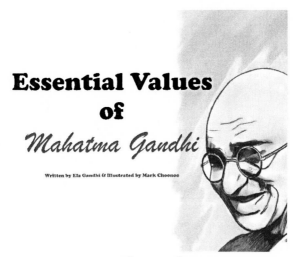

Ela's Book Cover

One corner of her mouth curled upward again in a grin. I could see a story forming in her head as her eye flitted up and down. "I don't know if I told you the story about the wild cat," she said.

"Not that I recall. I said. I pushed my chair back from the table and stretched out my legs.

I'm sure this is going to be interesting.

"When I was just about 9 years old, there was a wild cat that came to our yard at the Phoenix Settlement and this wild cat was on the top of our tree opposite the house. There were a whole lot of people living around the Settlement and they came with guns and wanted to shoot this cat. I was alone at home and they asked me for permission to shoot."

"Oh no," I said.

"I knew my parents would object, because they did not like guns and such kinds of force. But the neighbors from around the Settlement kept telling me the cat was going to cause damage, that he was a threat, and they needed to shoot it. And so, I said OK, and they shot it and took it away."

"That was unfortunate," said Dewey.

"So much pressure to put on a child," said Janice.

"When Mum and Dad came home, I told them what had happened. Today many parents would have gone to the neighbors and said, 'How can you come here and shoot an animal? You know that you aren't supposed to shoot on Phoenix Settlement.' But my parents did not. They made me understand that I was wrong giving that permission. Firstly, what did that cat do? 'Twas just a little baby cat and it wasn't harming anything. It would have gone away on its own. They asked me why I had given permission and reminded me it is a sin to shoot and to take life. They talked to me until I began to feel bad, and I couldn't sleep that night. I had nightmares about this cat."

Oh, Ela.

"The next day, I asked my mother, 'If I fast, will God forgive me?' My mother didn't excuse me and say, 'No, don't fast, you are still a child. You didn't know." She didn't defend me. She encouraged me to fast and to see if I felt forgiveness. And so, I fasted. As a young child, I took that fast and prayed about the shooting of the cat."

Harsh lesson.

It was a tiny incident in my life but when I think about it now, I see their intention. My parents didn't defend me. Today if you see kids making a mistake, the parents go to the school and defend their child. They excuse the child. They don't make the child accept responsibility. But my parents did, and I am so grateful for that because it taught me that you can forgive yourself and if you would learn to forgive yourself, you will be able learn to forgive other people."

"You learned from your mistake," I said.

"Yes, I learned that when I make a mistake, I can take responsibility for the mistake, and repent for the mistake, and know that other people make mistakes too, but we can learn to forgive each other."

"So, personal responsibility, forgiveness of yourself, and forgiveness of others go hand in hand, right?" I interrupted her. People were starting to fidget, looking at their watches, checking their plane tickets.

"Yes," she said. "And when you learn you can make a mistake and you can repent for a mistake, then you know that other people can also make mistakes. That was a great lesson in my life. And I'm so grateful that my parents made me face myself and the mistake I had made and didn't just tell me to forget about it. It was one little incident that meant a lot."

"That was a difficult lesson to learn," said Hayward. He was seated a few chairs down from us, leaning forward, listening to her story.

"Yes," said Ela. "But my parents did not need to punish me. I punished myself, which had more meaning to me than anything they could have done. I could have sat in the corner hating my parents or God, all kinds of things, which happens when people are excused from their mistakes. They taught me what was right and what was wrong and if you do a wrong, take responsibility for it and do something about it yourself."

"That's really powerful, Ela," said Gwen. "Susan is right. You really do need to write your autobiography."

Oh, thank you. A compatriot in my mission.

"I wouldn't know where to start." She repeated the answer she had given me several times before.

The time was drawing near for our departure. People were standing, stretching, shaking hands, hugging. None of us from the other hemisphere was looking forward to the grueling trip ahead. All of us had dozens of stories in our heads.

Out of the corner of my eye, I noticed Gwen, Lavern, and Ela in a tight, little circle, talking in hushed tones and glancing in our direction. They turned to us with an announcement.

"We are all sad to see this day arrive and this final visit end," said Lavern, "but we are pleased to inform you that Ela and I will be coming to Atlanta for a presentation at the University. We are looking forward to this and cannot wait to see you all again, this time in your wonderful city."

This news sparked a new energy in the room, as if someone turned the dimmer switch of our spirits back up to full on.

This isn't ending here and now. We were going to continue this fascinating chapter of our lives.

I walked Ela to the door with the thought of making one more pitch. "Ela," I said.

"Yes." Her head tilted downward but her eyes looked up at me, a kindly smile on her face.

She knows what I am going to ask.

"Would you please give some more thought to letting me help you write your autobiography? It would be such a contribution. Your experiences are so pertinent to what is happening in the world today."

"OK, Susan." Her lips were closed but the corners of her mouth pulled up in a grin. "I will give it some thought, and we can discuss it when I get to Atlanta."

Hallelujah! Miracles DO happen!

"Thank you. That's wonderful." My spirits lifted even more.

This wasn't ending yet. It was just an intermission.

Ela and I walked down the steps of the restaurant. I gave her a final hug. As she drove off, questions formed in my head.

I need to start writing these down before I forget them.

Our trip was already full of surprises but there were still a couple in store for us. At the airport, a friend from home, a seasoned Delta pilot, was among the crew flying our plane back to Atlanta. The plane was packed, no seat upgrades, but he gave us a tour of the cockpit and crew's quarters.

"Have you spoken with your son lately?" our pilot friend asked us. His voice held a tone of warning.

"Yikes, no," I said. "We've been so busy during our stay. We never called him, and he never said anything to us in his emails. Why?" Concern crept into our hearts.

"He's OK," he said. "But…"

But…? Not something a parent wants to hear about a 20-something daredevil son. Especially when he is a hemisphere away.

"But what?" we both said.

"He was in an ATV accident. He's fine," said our friend. "He came away with his dignity bruised, and he'll have a nice scar on his cheek for the rest of his life, but he'll survive."

Aaaaand, we're back to reality.

On the plane home, I wrote a list of questions to ask Ela. My plan had not changed. I would interview her, transcribe her answers, and give them to her to turn them into a book.

How difficult could that be?

We arrived safely in Atlanta, retrieved our bags, went through Customs, and took the shuttle to the parking lot. We hauled our suitcases to the car. I reached deep into the recesses of my purse to fish out my car keys. They weren't there. I opened my day bag.

No keys. I searched through my suitcase and briefcase. No keys. Dewey searched. No keys. I searched again. Still no keys.

I don't know how, and I don't know where, but my keys are back in KwaZulu Natal. Too bad my car is here in Atlanta. Drat!

We both sighed heavily. A frantic call to our son temporarily rectified the situation. He drove down from our hometown 80 miles from the airport with the spare key. We got to inspect the damage to his face.

Not as bad as my mother brain imagined.

He was happy to see us and forgave us the inconvenience. I pulled out of the airport and onto I-85.

"From start to finish," Dewey said, "our trip to South Africa was one surprise after another."

"That's an understatement," I said. "So many memories. And I cannot wait to see Ela and Lavern again."

And now I'll have to waste hours replacing all my keys.

Chapter 12

Principles

Ela's Life Principles

Principle 1   Take what is needed but take no more or you are depriving someone else.

Principle 2   Sacrifice for what you believe in. Do not submit to illicit means of getting what you want.

Principle 3   All life's works require discipline, determination, precision of thought and action, and economy of effort.

Principle 4   Ask for things that are achievable, then ask for the next thing.

Principle 5   See the dignity in doing work, no matter how mundane the work may be.

Principle 6   Care about all living things, human and animal, and be a good steward of Mother Earth.

Principle 7   Take personal responsibility for your actions. This is needed for humankind to move forward. Forgiveness of self and others is a component of personal responsibility.

Chapter 13

Ela in Atlanta

Is there no mercy in this world? It was August 2010, and we were back home in Georgia having breakfast. The topic of discussion was the horrors of apartheid. Dewey was finishing his breakfast. I was reading reports on the internet.

"It says here that the actions of the apartheid government were atrocious." I took a sip of my coffee. "They employed tactics of beatings, incarcerations, shootings, torture, and killings," I said, "including suffocation and electric shock."

Seriously? What is wrong with people?

"Yeah," said Dewey. "Remember when President Carter's daughter, Amy, was arrested for protesting Apartheid? Everyone knew about it here because Jimmy was from Georgia." He took his dishes to the sink.

"Amy was brave," I said. "The report says the younger victims were suffocated or submitted to severe electric shocks causing permanent mental disorders." I shoved myself away from the desk. "I will never understand how anyone can be cruel to children. What sick mind would think this was OK?"

Animals.

I closed out one website and opened the next. "This report says the South African police were implicated in most of the killings, beatings, and tortures," I said, "but that all the different police and military groups engaged in violence."

"Well," said Dewey, "they are all trained in how to be violent, so…" His voice trailed off. He poured himself another cup of coffee.

"It continues on," I said, "saying hundreds of men, women, and children were killed for protesting. Any uprisings were dealt with swiftly and violently." I swiveled in my chair toward him. "Can you imagine?"

"I'd rather not," he said.

"This next website says the 1980s were really bad," I said, "and the security forces used ambush techniques against people protesting in the streets." The cat started making circles around my feet. He wanted breakfast, too.

"Bystanders, including children," I said, "were often killed. And pretty much the streets were cruel and brutal places to be." I shut down the computer. "I can't look at this anymore," I said. "Gotta go play in the Atlanta traffic."

Once in the office, I could barely keep my mind on my academic duties.

Ela is flying into the Atlanta International Airport. These six months between our April trip to Durban and her October trip here flew by.

Ela and I had corresponded via email since our visit. She corrected me on an error.

RE: Next

(S) Susan

TO: Ela

Hi Ela,
Thank you for sharing so much with us about Gandhiji.

(EG) Ela Gandhi

TO: Susan

Ela: Pleasure. If you please, it would be correct for you to refer to him as Gandhi. 'Ji' is an endearment. Something a family member or beloved one would use.

RE: Next

 Susan

TO: Ela

Oh dear. I am sorry. Yes, I understand. Kind of like calling my father, Daddy. Not something a person working with him or writing about him would say.

 Ela Gandhi

TO: Susan

Quite

But emails were not the same. Written words rarely convey a person's light and energy.

I ran into Sue in the hallway, literally. We were rushing around the same corner, both preoccupied, heading in opposite directions. We shrieked, then laughed. The hallways of the institution with their cold walls were a far cry from the thriving ocean, luxurious grasslands, and rolling hills around Durban. "Another grant proposal due?" I said.

"Always," she said. "I wish you could join us for dinner tonight. M. L. King's daughter, Bernice, Congressman John Lewis, and Bernard Lafayette will be there. It's an impressive contingent of Civil Rights legends. They're all looking forward to meeting Ela."

"I know," I said. My voice dropped lower at the end of the sentence. "I am looking forward to seeing her again, but the paycheck doesn't make itself. Please give my apologies to Ela."

"No worries. She'll be here for a few days," said Sue. "There's a reception tonight in the Dean's conference room. You're coming, aren't you? And you'll be there for her presentation tomorrow night, and dinner at my house the next, right?"

"I wouldn't miss it for the world. See you later." I scurried off to my next meeting.

The reception began shortly after close of business. I could not wait to see Ela. Dewey is no fan of the 65-mile drive from our lake home to my office. "I'll make an exception," he said when I told him about the plans for the next few days. Even the Atlanta traffic could not dissuade him from a chance to talk with Ela again.

The reception room was packed with faculty and students. It was hard to hear anything above the din, but it was easy enough to find Ela at the head of the reception line. Tables with trays of cheese, crackers, fruits, vegetables, and dip were off to one side, the reception line off to the other. The Dean stood to her left, Lavern to her right. Dewey and I joined the line and waited our turn. We caught Ela's eye. She smiled quickly, then her eyes darted back to the person in the line with whom she was speaking.

The long line wound past some tables and chairs. We finally made it around the room.

"Susan, Dewey," Ela said. "It is so good to see you again." We exchanged quick hugs. The reception line was moving fast. I took her little hand between my two and gave it a pat.

"You must be exhausted from your flight," I said. We tried to hold our ground, but the crush of the line edged us forward.

"No, I am accustomed to traveling long distances. I can curl up and sleep most anywhere."

I forgot how tiny she is. Next to Lavern and the dean she looks itty bitty.

"That's fortunate, I have never been able to sleep on a plane." The momentum of the reception line moved us along, and we were soon looking backward at her.

"We'll see you tomorrow at the lecture," said Dewey. We waved, then he took a step back toward Ela, pulled me along, and asked someone to take our picture with her.

Short but sweet, just like Ela. Now back to business.

"I've gotta go to class," I said.

"I'm going to stay and see if I can visit some with Sue, Gwen, Hayward, and Lavern, the old traveling crew," said Dewey. "Call me when your class is over, and we'll head home."

I did not see Ela on the first day. She was adjusting to the time zone change and preparing to speak at the College of Education's 22nd annual Benjamin E. Mays lecture that evening. But I ran into Sue again.

"You really missed an interesting dinner last night," she said. "Ela, Lavern, Gwen, Bernice, John, Bernard, several folks from the Crim Center, and I had a wonderful time. We made a plan to take Ela on the Freedom Ride trail. We're taking a small busload down tomorrow. Can you join us?"

Nooo. Another missed opportunity.

"Sorry, but I have to sit on a tenure committee." A student of mine passed us and waved. "I would much rather go with you. There's nothing quite so painful as a tenure meeting."

"Oh, that's too bad," she said. "It promises to be an interesting trip." Her phone rang. She held up a finger, asking me to wait a minute before rushing off. She ended the call. "You're coming to the presentation tonight, right?" she said.

"Of course," I said. "Dewey, too. Save us a couple seats." We waved, both of us in our usual rush of the day.

That evening we gathered for Ela's presentation at the Speaker's Auditorium, a 413-seat venue with comfortable cloth seats. The place was packed. I went backstage to wish her luck.

"I hope this is meaningful for all those people out there. I am never comfortable with public speaking."

She sat in a chair, index finger riffling through her notes. Her fingers nervously wiped the corners of her mouth. She pulled a misbehaved shock of hair behind her ears, fidgeted with her garment. She wore a silky green blouse, short-sleeved, with a beige sari wrapped around her. It had a woven diamond design on it, one of those saris that can be worn both at casual and formal events.

"That's why we set up a question and answer format," I said. "All you need to do is answer from your heart."

Hmm. That's what Hayward told me before I spoke to the king and it worked out fine.

"I'm the same way, I would rather sit alone in a closet than stand in front of a group and speak, yet I ended up in a life that threw me in front of people. I'm sure you know the trick. Just find one kind face in the audience and talk to that person or talk to Donna."

The stage manager interrupted, motioning me to leave. It was showtime. Donna Lowry, WXIA TV personality, was already on the stage. She would ask the list of prepared questions. She was a polished interviewer. Her purple jacket shone brightly in the spotlight. The announcer introduced Ela. The spotlight moved from Donna to Ela, and she entered the stage to enthusiastic applause.

In all, the conversation ran for an hour and eight minutes. The depth and breadth of topics she covered were astounding. The crowd gathered around her as she walked down from the stage. One gentleman offered his hand to steady her on the steps. She politely accepted.

"Time for us to go, Ela," said Lavern. "Tomorrow will be a long day as we are replicating the Freedom Trail ride."

Like one of the pilot boat captains trained in his program at DUT, he skillfully maneuvered her around crowds of people who wanted to speak to her, thank her, touch her, take pictures with her. No one seemed to want her to leave. I understood the feeling. I made arrangements with the videographer to send me a link to the evenings' presentation.

Surely, she will agree to work on her autobiography if I type all this up and give it to her.

Ela left with a trail of people following. She gave me plenty to ponder as Dewey and I drove the 65 miles up the interstate to our home.

Chapter 14

Ela Speaks—The Atlanta Interview

It was October 4, 2010 and the auditorium was full. Ela and Donna were on the stage. Ela sat in the chair across a round table from Donna. On the table were two coffee mugs with the university logo on them. A single red rose sat between the cups in a glass vase. A beige banner with red symbols hung in the background. Ela clutched her sheets of paper in her left hand.

The crowd settled down, ready to listen to the conversation between Ela and Donna.

"Good evening," said Donna. "We are going to have a conversation this evening. I love this format. We're going to just sit here and talk. You can also write questions for Ms. Gandhi and pass them down the aisle to one of the ushers. They will gather them and bring them to the stage." The audience murmured.

Ela turned toward the audience. "Hello Everybody," she said, in that sweet, accented, slightly wavery voice.

"Hello," the entire audience said in unison. Their gentle response matched Ela's.

Awww. So sweet, both Ela and the crowd. This reminds me of a TV documentary I saw about Mr. Rogers. He started his presentation with "Hello Everybody," and they said "Hello," back. I can hear their fond childhood memories of Mr. Rogers in their softened voices.

Donna began the interview. "You grew up on the Phoenix Settlement," she said. "Your father was instrumental in bringing about the Freedom Charter, and of course, your grandfather was an icon. Would you please describe what life was like under Apartheid?"

"Gandhiji was inspired by the Mariannehill monastery," Ela said, "where all race groups worked together. Growing up at Phoenix

Settlement was very interesting because all these ideas were in place. Equality, respect for labor, self-sufficiency. We had enough to survive and enjoy our lives. The idea of accumulation meant you were depriving other people. This was in contrast to the fundamental beliefs of Apartheid."

Diametrically opposed.

"Apartheid was a terrible system. It discriminated on the basis of race. The system was entrenched by law. This gave credence to the system and they had laws to give justice to it." Ela held the fingers of her right hand together as if holding a flower which she was about to smell. She gestured at the audience in this manner.

"Apartheid was based on a false interpretation of religion," Ela said. "Religion taught that certain people were supposed to be masters and other people were supposed to be workers or laborers to serve those masters. This was entrenched in people through their religion. Every time they went to church, this was taught. That is why they looked upon Black people as inferior, and when I talk about black, I mean all those who are non-white. This is how it worked in South Africa (SA)."

She shifted back in her seat, her initial nervousness settling into a more comfortable demeanor. Her feet barely touching the floor.

"Living under that system was a nasty experience," said Ela. "All of us suffered. And we realized we had to do something about that oppression. There were restrictions on what we could do, where we could go. As in the U.S., we could not travel on the same bus as white people. We couldn't sit on a bench reserved for white people, even if there was nobody sitting there."

This is so familiar. So similar to what happened in the U.S. prior to Civil Rights.

"This was from my early childhood," she said, "and so we grew into this spirit of wanting to resist such control. This is what kept us going. Gandhiji's perspective encouraged us to address this in a non-violent way. And to build up our self-respect. The system took away our respect, so we had to build it within ourselves." She turned to Donna and leaned closer to her to hear her next question. Her eyes were wide open.

"I want to ask you to talk about the practice of banning and house arrest," said Donna. "In 1975 you were banned from participation in society and placed under house arrest for nine years. This is something this audience can't even imagine. But participation in activities against Apartheid received harsh punishment. How did you maintain your work, underground, so to speak? What was it like? And how did you keep your spirits up under these terrible, terrible conditions?"

Ela nodded at Donna, then turned to address the audience.

"I wasn't the only person under house arrest in South Africa," Ela said. "There were many, many people with banning orders and under house arrest. Many people were arrested for 90 days and over, for their political activities." She glanced down at the papers in her hand.

"It was really hard," she said. "I was about 30 years old at the time. My youngest child was three years old and my oldest was nine. And he was eighteen when the ban was lifted. So, his most formative years were spent under a ban with both his parents." She spoke this with a mother's tenderness for her suffering children.

"My husband was also banned, and house arrested," she said.

"Now, house arrest meant that from 7 o'clock at night to 7 o'clock in the morning during the week and from 5 o'clock on Friday afternoon to 7 o'clock on Monday, you could not leave the house. Even if your child was very sick. You had to ask someone to go get the doctor for you. And if you were out of food, or bread, or milk for the children, you had to ask someone to go get it for you. And we couldn't attend any social function, not even family functions. And the children grew up under those circumstances."

Concern tinged ever so slightly with indignation is in her otherwise calm voice. This has to be hard for her to talk about.

"Even today," she said, "you will see the scars of the bannings and arrests on my children and on other children of banned parents. But this was a price we knew we had to pay to fight against the injustice. And things could have been worse because many people were killed or incarcerated, so we were spared those alternatives. People were being tortured and murdered in prison. So, we had to accept what we had and to do whatever was necessary to keep our spirits up."

You could have heard a pin drop in the audience.

"I'd like to turn now to the idea of Affirmative Action," said Donna. "This was started in India by Mr. Ambedkar. Were you involved at all in that struggle?"

"Well, yes," said Ela. "I was very much involved in the gender struggle. One thing we always stressed when working on Affirmative Action is that women suffered a triple oppression. We suffered because we were poor, we suffered because we were women, and we suffered because we were black. All those things, poverty, gender, and race compounded the problem." Ela gestured with her hands or smoothed her dress while describing these experiences.

"We didn't really have a caste system the way it is practiced in India," she said. "Indians came to South Africa in 1860, and by the time I was growing up and politically aware in the 1950s, starting around the time I was 10, the caste system was subsiding. There were a lot of intermarriages and the caste system was going away."

Hmmm. Time to admit to a caste system in the US. The priest class, black and white, flies in multimillion-dollar planes. The administration and military class polices the world. The business class takes advantage of poor countries. Workers barely get by on a minimum wage. And our untouchables live on the streets.

"I want to talk a little bit now," Donna said, "about Gandhi's concepts of Ahimsa and Satyagraha. Tell us a little bit about what that means."

Ela nodded her head in agreement and turned to face the audience.

"Ahimsa means non-violence," she said, "but Ghandiji, you know, said it was more than non-violence. He described it as love. Martin Luther King from your city described it in a way people could understand. He used the word, "agape." Gandhiji agreed that ahimsa is love. It is the practice of trying to understand people, of loving them even if they are wrong, and of doing something to right the wrong. And that is what Satyagraha is all about. The basis of Ahimsa is love, and the basis of Satyagraha is non-violent love. He did not like the word, passive resistance. There is nothing passive about it. His resistance was very active." Ela became animated as she described her grandfather's approach. Her arms moved out toward the audience. Her eyes scanned the crowd more intently.

"When Gandhiji saw something wrong," she said, "he wanted to act against it. He wanted the people to understand the differences between aggression, passive resistance, and action. He felt a better word was needed. In order to get this new term, he asked readers of his newspaper, the *Indian Opinion*, to suggest a name. And that is how the term Satyagraha (sot-yuh-grah-hah) came out. The meaning of Satyagraha is the power of non-violence or the pursuit of non-violence. But it is broader, incorporating love and truth. It's just like the word Ubuntu, which is terminology used widely in Africa. Ubuntu simply means "I am because you are." Both Satyagraha and Ubuntu embrace community, compassion, love, and understanding—the Ubuntu way. These are very simple thoughts, but they take hours, or days, or a whole age to understand."

"It sounds like something we should try to understand," said Donna.

"Absolutely," said Ela.

"I am curious about the status of the indigenous Indians who are South Africans," said Donna.

"Well, the Dutch had brought Indians with them in the 17th and 18th centuries as slaves. The first Indian slaves were brought to Natal in 1849. In South Africa the race groups always fought together. We talked about ourselves as black. But we talked about more than that. We spoke about oppressed people. Even white people were oppressed. They were not allowed to sit on black benches or use their transport, even if it provided a better route. They had to go to white schools even if a black school was more convenient. So those people who were opposed to that system would classify themselves as black as well. That was our definition of black. Anyone who was oppressed was black."

There was a stirring in the audience.

Another new perspective.

"The relationship grew between our race groups through the struggle," she said. "We Indian people were very much involved in the struggle with people like Nelson Mandela and his right-hand man, Ahmed Kathrada. They were all in prison together. Many Indian people were in prison. It wasn't race forcing the people apart. Our slogan at the time was, 'Apartheid divides, UDF unites.'"

Good slogan. We are so divisive in this country.

"Apartheid divided us into all these superficial barriers and groups. Under the United Democratic Front (UDF), whatever color or race group, we were all united under this banner. Our unity was forged in action and it has survived to this day. Yes, there are problems. There were many xenophobic or racial attacks. These attacks are almost always contestations between the rich and the poor. In South Africa we have about 25% unemployment. There is a lot of poverty, a huge gap between the rich and poor. The conflict that appears to be xenophobia is almost always a contest for resources."

Not unlike the growing divide between the rich and the poor here, and the shrinking of the middle class.

"Let's get back a bit to your thoughts on non-violent resistance and dispute resolution," said Donna. "When did you first become aware of resistance? I call it 'passive resistance,' but you told me…"

"…Satyagraha."

"Yeah," said Donna. "Tell me your thoughts on that."

"Well, I grew into it," said Ela, "because in our family and at Phoenix Settlement, we did three things there. One was a simple lifestyle. I spoke of this. The other was, a newspaper and my father and grandfather kept the community informed and mobilized that way. The third thing is my father and grandfather were involved politically. My mother, Sushila, and grandmother, Kasturba, were also highly involved in mobilizing the community against Apartheid. I was raised in it, grew up in it, steeped in it. There was no one moment when I became aware of it. I can tell you one story, though. I had a disagreement with my parents about whether they would school me, or I would go to school. I wanted to join my friends in the neighborhood, so I protested."

The audience laughed. *I can just see her standing there, stamping her little foot.*

"That was my first Satyagraha," she said. "That's when I first practiced my own resistance. And one little victory gives you the strength for the next resistance." Ela tilted her head back and chuckled. The audience laughed along with Ela.

"You found your own voice," said Donna.

"Yes," she said.

"We have talked about Gandhi," Donna said. "Martin Luther King, Jr., Nelson Mandela, and Lech Walesa in Poland all held similar views. Do you believe these principles are still relevant today?"

"Absolutely, I think today the world is facing many problems. Thousands of people are dying daily because of hunger, lack of accommodations, no access to healthcare, no access to simple, clean drinking water. Everyday thousands of people die in the world just because of that. In a situation like that, there is volatility. People get angry. They want to fight but by taking on Ghandiji's principles and by using non-violent means, there's far greater chance of success. There is far greater chance of getting the support of the world for their struggles, and therefore I think that his philosophy is absolutely relevant today, more than ever before."

I couldn't agree more. Protests still pop up in the US over long-standing issues of racial and gender equality. But pop-up protests die down. Maybe if people could hear Ela's suggestions, protests would be more productive.

"And the world is becoming more violent and more polarized," she said. "There are more deaths, which could be prevented. We used to talk about millionaires. Today we talk about billionaires and one day we will be talking about trillionaires. But what about the poor? What's happening to them? There are more and more poor people in the world. In that kind of society, Ghandiji's philosophy is absolutely relevant because if those millionaires and billionaires would share, today there would be no need for people to be without shelter, without water, without food, and without access to healthcare."

The audience broke out into applause. Several of the student members of the audience rose to their feet. She and Donna smiled at each other.

"You have had many achievements," said Donna. "Let me just read some of them here. You were an executive member of the Natal Organisation of Women from its inception until 1991. You were affiliated politically with the Natal Indian Congress, and served as vice president. You were also active in the United Democratic Front, the Descom Crisis Network, and the Inanda Support Committee. When Apartheid ended, you were a member of the Transitional Executive Council. More recently you were President of the World Council of Religions for Peace. As a member of that Council, you participated on the United Nations Millennial Goals Committee, correct? And the list of your awards during all this activism is as long as my arm. That brings me to this beautiful banner behind us that you received earlier this week. Tell us about it."

"Well," Ela said, "the World Council of Religions for Peace organized young people from around the world to act for peace. These people come from all over the world, young people, students, who got together and started a campaign called 'Down with Arms.' And in this campaign what they are saying is, 'let us ask our governments to reduce the budget on defense by just 10% over a period of time, by just 10% of the money they use'. And they use about 1.5 trillion U.S. dollars on defense. This is collectively. The world uses that much of money on defense. Now if you took 10% of that and put it in the millennium development goals, then people will have access to that water, to their healthcare, to housing and so on. Those are some of the millennium goals."

That's a tall order, to get politicians to let go of the money they have their hands on.

"And so," she said, "the young people went out and started the campaign. It was launched in Costa Rice and I think professor Lafeyette would know about that. It was Dr. Arias, Oscar Arias, the former president of Costa Rica who launched the campaign there, and then it was taken on by these young people. Now, they collected 20 million signatures, which were given to the Secretary General of the United Nations on Monday. The National Day of Non-Violence happened to be on Saturday so on the Monday they gave these petitions to the Secretary General. In Japan they collected eleven million signatures. They were told by some of the believers there that if you go to every one of our 88 temples, which are situated in the whole of Japan, whatever campaign you are running will be successful. So, they decided to go to the 88 temples. Look at the banner on the wall behind us." She turned around in her chair, motioning to the banner on the wall.

"On that banner is the stamp of each one of those 88 temples. They spoke to the followers of that temple and asked them to sign the petition. They went out to each individual and asked them to sign the petition that they gave to the Secretary General. That's how they collected 11 million signatures and then also went to those 88 temples."

Murmurings were heard from the audience.

"I know you were honored to receive that banner," Donna said.

"Absolutely," said Ela. "'Twas a wonderful experience, it is very moving, and it showed the power of the young people. When channeled in the correct direction, young people are the future of tomorrow and I thought it was beautiful. I think it's a campaign that has just started and I would invite the young people here to join the campaign. I think we have problems with the budget cuts. Our education budgets in my country have been cut, in your country, the same situation. And the people who suffer are the poorest of the poor who should have access to education. But because of the budget cuts they may be deprived of that access to education. So, let's all of us get together and say it is important that we have good education, we have shelter, healthcare facilities and so on than to have more guns and more nuclear weapons and armaments."

This raised more applause from the crowd.

"Beautifully said. Thank you for sharing that with us, bringing that here," said Donna. "I want to get back to a little bit in the history. You were among a select few members of the United Democratic Front who met with Nelson Mandela prior to his release from Pollsmoor Prison on February 11, 1990. What was the atmosphere surrounding those meetings just prior to his release?"

"I feel truly blessed, that I was given that opportunity to be there in that delegation. I am not one of those great leaders of South Africa. I am one of the small activists who took part in the struggle. But to be chosen to go in that last delegation was indeed an experience that I will cherish for the rest of my life. Prior to Mr. Mandela's release, other famous activists were released. People were coming back from exile, so the spirit was very high in the country at that time. Everyone was now just waiting for Mr. Mandela to come out and for something to happen in our country to give us the freedom that we wanted."

I can tell this is a fond memory for her. Her smile gets broader and broader the more she talks about this experience.

"We were at the threshold of getting our independence, one person one vote, and one parliament for all the people. So, there was a euphoria and to be able to go and meet Mr. Mandela on the eve of his release, I can't describe it, it was so wonderful. I feel so blessed. As I feel blessed that I am in the Gandhi family. I must have done something really wonderful in my past life."

The audience laughed. Her smile during this segment of the discussion was contagious. Applause broke out. She turned to the audience again and acknowledged their laughter with a slight bowing of her head.

"You're definitely doing wonderful things," said Donna, "and we feel blessed to have you here. I mentioned that you were also a member of the Transitional Executive Committee at the end of Apartheid so what were your primary challenges for that role because we were watching from afar, from over here when all of that was going on. What was it like to be in the midst of all the change?"

"OK," said Ela. "There were a number of challenges we faced during that time. It was four months before the elections. We had to make sure that everybody, you know, goes to the polls. We wanted a large turn out and we had to educate the people about elections. How to get to the polls, how to elect, how to set up a campaign, how to ensure the election was free and fair. All those things were part of the challenge. But the biggest challenge we faced was to ensure a fair election. Someone had to watch for acts of violence. Someone had to watch for people trying to manipulate others' votes in illegal ways because we all know that they do. So, we had to ensure it was fair and free. To do that, we needed the army and the police to play a big role."

More excellent suggestions. I hope the young activists in this crowd are taking notes.

"Now," she said, "the army there was a South African army from in the Apartheid government, and the police force belonged to the previous government. Would they, you know, protect the people? Would they protect the integrity of the election? These were some of the challenges we faced. But at the same time when our people returned, there were other armies as well. These armies were fighting with each other previously, like the uMkhonto we Sizwe (pronounced u'mk^{h}onto we 'sizwe) army, which was the African National Committee's army. When we came back there were armies that were fighting, and we had to bring them together during the time of the Transitional Executive Council. We had to make sure they worked together, not as enemies but as protectors. And they had to work together in cooperation and protect the community. We had to change that mindset. Previous armies looked at people in terms of race, they looked at people in terms of gender divisions and that had to change as well."

The diplomacy, tact, and skills of persuasion required to do this must have exhausted her. I see how she could have pulled that off, with her gentle and quiet ways. Not at all threatening or aggressive. In the right place at the right time in history.

"So," she said, "we looked at their rules and regulations. It was a real challenge, I can tell you, sitting with the generals of the army. They didn't even think we women existed. When they talked, they would say, 'Gentlemen this' and 'Gentlemen that.' But here I was, a woman and I wondered, 'Why won't you talk to me as well?' But this is how it happened in that time. One time a general blamed women for not becoming more like men. I said, 'I have to challenge you on that. Women are equally as strong as men and can be leaders in their own right. They don't have to become men to be strong.' Needless to say, the room became very quiet." Laughter erupted from the audience. Her lips tensed, bold and resolute, but pleased with the response.

"We had to change their mindsets," she said. "Women were present, and women were also going to occupy senior positions. In uMkhonto we Sizwe we had women who were also generals. And they were going to be sitting side by side with other generals. We had to get them to change their mindsets and to accept this new situation and that was a huge challenge. I can tell you we worked together. We were calm and resolute. They could not provoke us. And well, eventually we did convince them. But I always did my homework and knew more about the documents under discussion than some of the men."

Why does this not surprise me?

"I know one little story," she said, "where they told me that women were never going to be allowed to sit in a submarine. They showed us all the armaments they had. One of the places they took us to was the submarine. When we looked at this it was designed only for men. There were no facilities and when we asked them 'Where will the women be in this place?' they said, 'No, no, we protect our women. We can't expose them to these conditions.' And so, I asked, 'Why shouldn't women be allowed? What about the women who want to be here? Why is there discrimination?' They did not have an answer to that one. Today Dr. Samuels at DUT has a number of students who are part of the Navy and they come to train there and amongst them are women. They had to change the submarines to make them gender friendly."

More laughter from the audience.

"You stood your ground," said Donna.

"Absolutely," Ela said.

"I am curious now about the decade between 1994 and 2004," said Donna, "coming out of all of that, during which you were a member of parliament immediately after the end of Apartheid. Tell us about that."

"Well, parliament in the first five years was a real challenge and it was very, very interesting because the laws and the conditions in parliament were set there by the Apartheid government. We had to change all those laws, so we looked at thousands of laws. I can't remember the number of laws we changed in the first five years, but I think we set a record."

More laughter from the audience. Soft and light this time.

"I am not sure whether it was a world record," she said, "but certainly in South Africa there was a large number of amendments that were scrapped, and new laws were brought into their position. This is because of the change in complete thinking from Apartheid to the democracy that we wanted to see. The second thing was that parliament had to be friendly to people."

Good luck.

"Previously," she said, "it was a parliament that was very elitist in the sense that they made the laws, they knew what the laws should be, what kind of laws the people needed. They didn't need to listen to what the people had to say. That was the mentality in those days, and when we got in parliament, we wanted to listen to people. We wanted people to come and interact with parliamentarians, so we threw the doors of parliament open and that was a huge challenge, ensuring people come in. And today you can go straight into parliament. You can visit people and you can, you know, make your contributions in the different laws processes and so on, but that started in that first five years."

Such sweeping changes not only to the mindset of those who wanted it, but to the mindset of those who resented it and still opposed it. I'm sure that was lying under the surface. Not unlike folks here who still insist on flying the Confederate flag. I have news for them. The South already rose, they just missed the boat. Thirty-four percent of the nation lives in the South. All the major corporations are here. We have one of the largest international airports in the world.

"And the challenge," said Ela, "was for us who really didn't know how parliament works, because it was the first time we got into parliament and we had to find our way and assert ourselves when they told us, 'Hey, it doesn't work like this, you can't allow those people to come in here, you are going to cause chaos in parliament.'"

A fearful time for the old guard, too.

"We said, 'no we have to get them here and we have to find a system whereby they come in, so you don't have anarchy. They can't accuse us of causing anarchy in the parliament. To ensure our ideas and values are respected in parliament.' So, this is what we had to do in the first five years. And it was very interesting and very empowering for us. We also brought in the new constitution with the beautiful Bill of Rights which we are all very proud of in South Africa. The constitution, the Bill of Rights which are embodied in the constitution, and our Human Rights Commission. We passed the law in the first five years. And the Truth and Reconciliation Commission, although we do see there are weaknesses now in hindsight, but it was challenging work and it was empowering."

"So much wonderful history," said Donna. "I know there are people in the audience who have questions. We asked them to write them on cards and then pass them down to the end of the rows. Here are my cards. Let's look at the first question.

"OK. Here is one. President Carter and others have used the word Apartheid to describe the current oppression of the Palestinian people under Israeli occupation. Your description of South African

Apartheid certainly has strong connections with the current situation in Israel Palestine. What is your perception of this connection and the use of the word apartheid in that context?"

"Oppression is oppression," said Ela, "no matter where, whether it's in the state or whether it is in any other country. Oppression is felt by the people in many different ways and Israeli government in many different ways is oppressing Palestine or the people of Palestine by depriving them of water, because they are landlocked there, by depriving them of many other facilities and so on. But they are not ruling over Palestine. It's not one state where you have a government that is ruling over another people and discriminating against them."

"Here is the next question," said Donna. "What would you suggest for the next generation to focus on in today's social struggles? You talked about the disarmament. That and any other social issues you think the young people should be involved with."

"I think the young people face a huge challenge at the moment, because of the way the world is moving. We are all concerned about the fragile nature of the planet. We don't know what is going to happen in the next century. Whether we are going to have sufficient resources, drinking water for the people. There are those people that say the next war will be about drinking water, access to drinking water. Food, water, energy, climate change, all of these are challenges. The next generation needs to focus on less destructive ways than destroying or burning up scarce resources. By destroying those facilities, you are depriving other people access to them."

"Can I ask you about an education issue because I cover education for the TV news," said Donna. "What do you think about education today and the future of education in South Africa? I think given what we are dealing with in education here in this country it is an important question?"

"We had a huge challenge changing the education system from the time the Apartheid system was in place until today. We still haven't achieved our goals. Look at some of our history lessons, for example. They don't record our struggle. It was largely hidden. People don't know about it, and it can be lost completely to the people of the next generation unless we have people recording that history of the struggle. That's one part of it but the other part is, there was a philosophy that was behind Apartheid. How far have we changed that philosophy and put in its place the philosophy that informed our liberation struggle? And that's a challenge because until we change that philosophy, who is going to apply new methodologies and with what mindset? So that has to change."

"And you're not there yet," said Donna.

"No," said Ela. "We're not there yet."

"Here's another question," said Donna. "What sort of political, social, and economic conditions should exist to facilitate the emergence of a Gandhi-like leader today? Should there be one?"

"Well, I don't know," said Ela. "They do say that adversity leads to leadership. But it's not necessary that you have to have adversity, or you have to have those condition in order to bring into being a leader of the stature of Gandhiji. I think today there are many leaders we have seen coming up in various parts of the world, young people who may not have reached the level of Gandhiji but in their own way have contributed to the struggle. We talk about people like Vandana Shiva, food sovereignty advocate, who is struggling to ensure that organic foods are available to people. There are others in the world of social reform coming up and talking about things. So, I think, you know, the world will see leaders coming up. You don't have to have major disasters to bring about a leader. We will have them."

"I could sit here and talk with you for a lot longer," said Donna, "but it looks like we have run out of time. I want to thank you so much for being here today. I know this audience has enjoyed having you here. You have given us so much to think about and really believe in and I want to thank you for that so please stand and receive this warm applause from this audience."

The applause was genuinely warm with some whistles included.

Chapter 15

Ela on the Freedom Trail

"I t's taking forever to get to Sue's house," Dewey said. "How much longer?"

We were driving on the I-285 perimeter, a particularly unpleasant stretch of 8 to 10-lane highway that rings Atlanta. Our house was to the northeast of the city. Sue and her husband, Robert's, to the southwest. Might as well have been in another state.

"This is going to be a fun dinner with Ela," said Dewey. He grinned from ear to ear.

"Next time we do this," I said, "we need to take a helicopter. This traffic is brutal."

Nothing's quite so comforting as skimming 70 miles an hour down the interstate escorted by a tractor-trailer truck on either side. And now we have more construction. What else is new?

"This road construction is going to make us late," I said. I looked cautiously in all rearview and side mirrors, hoping to merge safely into the single lane skirting the construction.

Every. Single. Time.

"There's always road construction in Atlanta," said Dewey. He fumbled with the radio knobs and found a station with Beatles music, still his favorite group.

"Would you call Sue on my Blackberry and tell her what's holding us up?" I said. I was gripping the wheel like a trapeze artist with no net below.

"Sure," he said.

♪♫ "It's been a hard day's night, And I've been working like a dog. It's been a hard day's night, I should be sleeping like a log" receded into the background as Dewey turned down the radio. He fished the phone out of my purse, typed in Sue's number, and placed the call.

"Hi Sue," he said. "This is Dewey."

"Let me guess," she said. Her voice exaggerating the words, then finally hammering down on "Construction."

"Yep, always," he said. "But we're passed it now."

"Tell Susan she missed a great trip," she said. "We went with Ela on the Freedom Ride Trail. It was an amazing day." We hit a cell tower dead zone and lost contact for a few seconds, but the signal returned.

"I'm going to regret missing that one for a long time," I said to Dewey. "Ask her how many of them went."

"She says twelve of them," he said. He held the phone to my ear. I listened to Sue's comment.

"First, we went to Tuskegee, Alabama, to visit the Tuskegee Institute National Historic Site," she said. "Ela was excited to see it because it is a historically Black college and so connected to the Gandhi philosophy."

"Home of the World War II Tuskegee Airmen," I said.

"Yes, and when we got there, the Mayor of Tuskegee gave Ela the key to the city," Sue said.

"Ela must have been so pleased," I said.

"Yes," Sue said. "She was very touched to see the university where George Washington Carver did all his experiments. Grandfather Gandhi corresponded with Carver, and Carver advised Gandhi on agriculture and nutrition. But I'll let her tell you about it when you get here."

"Great," I said. "We're just about to get off 285." The muscles in my neck and shoulders relaxed a bit.

"Hey, Dewey," Sue said. "You have the cake, right?"

"Yes," he said. "And I have a little surprise on it for Ela."

The call ended. Dewey tossed the phone back into my purse.

We arrived at Sue and Robert's mid-century modern home atop a small mountain. The view of downtown Atlanta was impressive. Dewey grabbed the cake out of the trunk, and we went inside.

"Other than the fact that you are bringing one," I said, "does Sue know about the cake?"

"No, just you," he said. He balanced the large cake on his knee as he shut the car door. Cars were parked close together all up and down the street.

Popular place to be this evening.

We walked up the tree-lined drive and into the house. People were everywhere, in all the rooms, both inside and outside the house.

I knew there would be a huge turnout. Ela's Benjamin Mays presentation was a real hit, not to mention the fact that Sue throws the best parties.

We stopped in the kitchen to deposit Dewey's cake. The traveling group was there—Sue, of course, Gwen, Hayward, and Janice. Hugs were had all around. Glasses clinked, laughter wafted in from poolside through a door opened between the living room and patio. Lively conversation abounded.

Yes, another great Sue party.

Wild laughter floated in from the pool area beyond the patio. It caught my attention and I looked in that direction. I noticed Ela and Lavern standing near one of the large glass doors leading outside.

"Let's go say hi to them," I said to Dewey. Once again, she was surrounded with people waiting their turn to talk with her. Lines of people were walking past, asking for pictures with her.

"Hello, again," I said. "That was such a wonderful presentation last night. Sue started to tell us about your trip. I would love to hear more about it. Come here. Let's sit down."

I walked over to the sofa, sat down and patted it, hoping she would join me. She looked tired. It had been a long drive to Selma and back. She came over and sank into the deep cushions. A pianist was playing music on Sue's baby grand at the other end of the room. "Is this your first time to Atlanta?"

"No, I was once here some time ago with the Parliamentary delegation. This was my first time away from the city, though. The trip to Tuskegee was just mind-boggling."

"I heard you went to the Rosa Parks Museum," I said, "in Montgomery, Alabama. Sue said they had an exhibit on the Montgomery Bus Boycott. I had always thought of Rosa as an older woman, but she was still quite young when that happened. Only 42, and tired from her long day as a seamstress. I know her arrest is credited with starting the Civil Rights Movement in the United States." The pianist finished a jazz piece and move onto some easy listening tunes.

"I was so taken up with that," Ela said, "to see where Rosa Parks lived, because we used to talk about her during our women's meetings while we were planning our activism. She was a role model for us. When I saw the museum and I saw the kinds of things that Rosa Parks did, it was a moving experience."

"And not unlike what you described in Apartheid South Africa," I said. "Separate buses, drinking fountains, bathrooms, and schools for African Americans and whites."

"Yes," she said. "There was a replica of the bus she rode on the day she refused to give up her seat. I enjoyed walking through the bus. It must have taken so much courage to stand up to the bus driver, the white passengers, and the police."

She must be experiencing déjà vu. So reminiscent of her own experiences at the hands of the police.

"Where did you go next?"

"To Selma, Alabama," she said, "where Martin Luther King, Jr. began his historic march. To me, it was so touching to see the struggle to vote. They said in 1965, only 2% of the eligible African American voters were successfully registered. The first time they tried to cross the Edmund Pettus Bridge, as you know, there was a terrible clash. Bloody Sunday, and this reminded me so much of the carnage Gandhiji experienced during the Salt March in India. Luckily, the second attempt was successful because U.S. Army troops and the National Guard attended them. So now you've got the Voting Rights Act."

"The parallels between 1965 in the southern U.S. and 1997 in South Africa are really striking," I said. "And Gandhi is linked to both struggles."

"Yes," said Ela. "There is still such a need for nonviolent responses to political inequalities. So much need for support of the poor."

So soft-spoken, such weighty words. Must be burdensome at times to carry the legacy of her grandfather in a world that has both progressed and regressed. We still have barely veiled segregation, voter intimidation, unexplained deaths, and violence from extremists in both of our countries.

"Your family fought so hard to dismantle Apartheid," I said.

"Yes," she said. "And we will continue to fight the good fight, to see equality and justice for all people until the last."

Suddenly all heads turned to the kitchen as Dewey's shot-gun blast laugh reverberated through the crowd.

"I never have to wonder where Dewey is," I said to Ela. "I just listen for the laugh. He can be on the other side of Home Depot and I just have to walk in the direction of the laugh."

This brought a giggle up through Ela's throat. She hunched her shoulders up, as if trying to keep it from becoming a full-fledged laugh.

"And did you get to meet any other Civil Rights leaders?" I said.

"Well, yes and no," she said. We went to the home of Amelia Boynton. She fought for voter's rights and was brutally beaten on the Pettus bridge. She was around 99 years old. I was very disappointed that she wasn't there. I have heard her speeches. She said, 'You have to go and exercise your vote.' That was really wonderful. A person even that age being so powerful, so precise in what she thinks is important in life. Obviously, she felt that voting was an important responsibility. She didn't tell people they should go and work and earn a lot of money, or go to Disneyland, she told them go and vote."

Important advice today.

"You understand the importance, and now people have the right to vote," she said. "That generation struggled for the right, and now future generations must exercise it. The young people in the museum were so enthusiastic as they showed us around. I saw the cell in which Dr. Lafayette was held, the little cell, and it was so reminiscent of the cell in which Mr. Mandela had the same experiences, so it was very enlightening."

"That's the no part," I said. "What was the yes part?"

"One of the people I was hoping to meet while in Atlanta," said Ela, "was Andrew Young, but his schedule would not permit him to join us at dinner. When we walked up to the steps of Amelia's house, I was flabbergasted. Sitting right there on the steps totally by coincidence was Andrew Young. Turns out he was scheduled to be in Selma. I will truly never forget that moment."

"Yes, I heard someone say the two of you had so much admiration for each other. She said the regard you two historical icons shared was palpable."

"Oh my," said Ela. "Well, there was only one icon. Not me. I did not contribute as much to our cause as Young did to his."

She is just way too modest. But that's part of her charm. The saying about water being soft and silent yet carving out canyons certainly applies to her. A strong gale can topple a sailboat, but a gentle breeze guides it safely to port, no matter the time and distance required.

"May I have your attention, please," said Sue. In the kitchen, she clinked her glass with a spoon. The sunken living room of her home placed her as if she were on a stage, higher than her guests. It took attacking the glass several more times for the conversations among the partygoers to die down. The music from the piano ceased.

"Good evening," Sue said. "Thank you all for coming to share this evening with Ela. We have a treat for you. Please welcome Dr. Lavern Samuels from DUT."

Ever regal in bearing, head high, neck straight, shoulders back, he moved forward to stand beside Sue. Polite applause circled around the room and wafted in from the patio. Someone's Blackberry rang, diverting the attention of the crowd. A mumbled, embarrassed apology followed.

"Lavern is going to tell ya'll about a special dish that was developed in the 1940s in Durban," Sue said. "It's called 'Bunny Chow.'" She turned and said, "Take it away, Lavern."

More applause. People from the patio moved inside. Standing room was at a premium. The air was getting close, but every so often a cool breeze from the patio drifted in. Sweet with the fragrance of a late-blooming blue mistflower, it restored the air.

"Thank you, Sue," Lavern said. "It is an honor and a delight to be here in Atlanta. Ela and I have been warmed by the generous way you have taken us into your hearts, homes, and cultures. It is, then, my pleasure to share with you this epicurean treat from the Indian South African community in Durban."

He stood erect, chest forward, hand out, palm up. It reminded me of all the orations we had seen while in South Africa. Formal speeches, none of the off-the-cuff, homespun, aw-shucks commentary that is the style today in the US.

"Bunny chow is easy to prepare," he said. "It is a curried dish, originally vegetable, but more recently lamb or beef have been included. It is served within a bowl cut out of a loaf of white bread. The first ever take-away fast food." This brought ripples of laughter, smiles, winks, and nods from the crowd.

"I invite those of you who would like a cooking lesson into the kitchen." He turned to Sue, yielding the floor. He lifted his chin to the side and bowed to the audience, acknowledging their applause.

Finally, dinner time arrived. The smells from the kitchen made mouths water. Classic Southern food mixed with the spicy fragrance of curry. In addition to bunny chow, there was chicken, vegetable salads, pasta salads, turkey or ham on small buns, and the ubiquitous Southern sweet tea. This kept everyone busy for a while.

Sue pulled Dewey into the kitchen. They returned with a large sheet cake. He uncovered it and she got a glimpse of the outline on the cake. White frosting with a black outline of Gandhi.

"How did you do that?" she said. Eyes wide.

"I went to www.gdt.org/za and found the picture of Gandhi's robe in the shape of India. Ela told me about it. I took the picture to Publix and talked the baker into putting it on a sheet cake."

After the cake was served and some clean-up attended to, I searched for Ela. I found her sitting outside on the patio at a round table and looking out over the Atlanta skyline.

"May I join you?" I said. It was time to bring the autobiography question up again.

"Pleasure," said Ela. She looked up at me from her seat and waved an arm toward the empty chairs.

"You must be exhausted by now. You've had quite the schedule. I sat in the chair beside her, leaning my elbow on the table, turning toward her.

"Tell me about the trip to Tuskegee. What did you think of it?" I said.

"It was a very enlightening experience," said Ela, "because I saw the theories, the philosophy of Gandhiji in the life of Washington Carver, who invented all sorts of things from peanuts. He strongly believed in the importance of rural agriculture, and that's exactly what Gandhiji believed in. Everybody can't just go to the city. You have to have the city and you have to have the farm," she said, "and you have to develop them to be equally as attractive."

Such irony. We're in this elegant home on a mountainside overlooking the lights of the city. And she is tired and longing to go back home, or at least to go to sleep. The jet lag alone would do me in.

"I thought it was very important to see the museum," she said, "to have it explained to me and to compare it with my grandfather's ideas. I found a synergy between the two experiences. Coming from South Africa and seeing the struggle for equality there and in the U.S., there's a common heritage, a shared history between us, and going to Dr. King's memorial was an emotional and educational experience. They let me place a wreath around Gandhiji's statue. Now I've seen where it all started."

We paused as an airplane went overhead on its path toward Hartsfield International Airport.

"Ela," I said. "On the day we left Durban, you said you would think about letting me help you write your autobiography. Do you remember that?"

Please, please, please remember the conversation.

"Yes," she said. "I don't know what I was thinking. I wouldn't know where to start."

"I can write up the stories you told me in South Africa. We also have the video from your presentation at the university. And next year, when Gwen, Sue, and I come back to Durban, if you are willing, I can interview you. I started a list of questions on the plane ride back to Atlanta. I can transcribe the interview. Then you can just choose the parts you want to share and put them together in a collection of stories. I would be happy to help you with that."

Perhaps I had worn her down. Perhaps she was just exhausted and there was no resistance left, passive or otherwise.

"OK, yes," she said. Her voice was quiet. "We can do that next time you are in Durban."

"Thank you," I said. "You have so much to share. How difficult can it be?"

Up on this mountainside, her agreement had me on top of the world.

Chapter 16

Visiting Bapu

"There it is, Gwen," I said. "There's the FIFA stadium."

It was March 3, 2011, and I was flying into the Durban airport for my second visit and another round of interviews. Durban was one of the sites where the Fédération Internationale de Football Association held its 2010 games. Our April 2010 trip put us there too early to see the games.

"Yes," said Gwen. "It's too bad we couldn't have timed our trips differently. It's OK, though. We have plenty to keep us busy for a while."

Our taxi took us to a hotel this time. We opted for one with an ocean view rather than another B&B.

"It's exciting to drive past familiar territory," I said. "A year is a long time to be away, but I remember it like it was yesterday." I leaned forward, peering out the windows, waiting for familiar landmarks. The highways were still as congested with traffic, the hills still gave way to informal housing, and informal housing to the city."

"There's the Elangeni hotel," said Sue. "Look how close we are to the ocean. Just across the street."

"Still a wilder ocean than I'm used to on the east coast of the U.S.," I said.

The hotel was a high-rise and very modern. A doorman in a red uniform met us at the taxi. A receptionist in the lobby offered us lemon water.

"It's late, said Gwen, "so let's just call it a night."

A bellman escorted us up the elevator, depositing us and our belongings in our separate rooms.

"We'll call you in the morning around 7:30 and decide where to meet for breakfast," said Sue. Her shoulders were low. She looked as tired as I felt.

"Perfect," I said. "Don't forget I'm supposed to be at Ela's flat around 10 tomorrow for our first interview."

"How could we," said Gwen. "You've been talking about it for months." She gave me a friendly nudge with her elbow.

The next morning at 9:30 a taxi drove me to Ela's flat. Tons of paper and pens joined a Sony mini recorder, a dozen micro-cassettes, and a Flip Camera in my carrying case.

I don't want to miss a thing. If I record her from multiple angles, I should be OK.

Ela opened the door. She wore a lovely beige dress with black, white, and brown flowers embroidered onto the sleeves, shoulder, and hem. "Welcome," she said. We exchanged hugs. "Come in. Do set your bags down on the table." Her eyes were wide open and staring at me, at my bag, and at me again.

She's nervous. Don't scare her off, now. You've come this far.

"Would you like some tea?" she said.

Would I? None of the brands of chai tea I tried at home measured up the tea you made last time I was here.

"Yes, ma'am. That would be wonderful."

As she went about pouring the tea, I set up the audio-and video-recorders on the dining room table. She placed the cup of tea in front of me. It was every bit as warm and spicy as I remembered. We exchanged chitty chat. She sat at table's end, facing out the window. I sat diagonally to her left, facing the door. This time I noticed her glasses. Wire-rimmed like Grandfather Gandhi's but rectangular in shape, not round.

I don't know why this makes me smile. Other than that, not much has changed in this past year, and I get a second chance to look at her artifacts.

The interview started shortly after 10:15. "Thank you, again for agreeing to do this," I said. "I'm not sure how I got so lucky as to be the one to interview you. Your life has been so interesting, you should have a professional biographer."

"Oh, no." She shook her head and gave me one of her closed mouth smiles, head down, eyebrows raised.

"We can take as many breaks as you would like," I said, "and if there is a question you don't want to answer, we can circle back to it, or we can drop it. It's up to you."

"That's fine, thank you," she said. "We can begin."

"I want to start by asking you what your objective is for allowing me to do this. My objective is to help you write your autobiography so people can learn about you and about the work of the Gandhi Development Trust and its continued efforts. But what do you hope the result of this will be?"

"Yes," she said, "the work. And if I can get Gandhi's message out to the world, that would be wonderful."

"When I was here last year," I said, "you told me a story about your early years, up to about age nine. I want to pick up there, but a question has been on my mind since the beginning."

Ela nodded her head in assent.

"Gandhi returned to India before you were born," I said. "Did you ever get a chance to see him face to face?"

"Oh my, yes," she said. "As a child of 7, amidst the events surrounding Partition and the Independence of India, my parents and I visited Bapuji's ashram. When I went to the Sevagram Ashram in India with my mom, it was the first time I met my grandfather. I was quite excited about the visit. My dad and brother also accompanied us, but I remember they had different living quarters. Soon after arriving I found that the daily lunch menu comprised of boiled pumpkin, some curds of yogurt, roti, and home-made butter."

"What is roti?" I asked.

"A flat-bread made from stoneground wheat and water," Ela said. "After eating this meal for a few days, at one of our regular meetings with my grandfather, I asked him why he had named the ashram 'Sevagram'. He explained that 'Seva' meant 'service' and "gram" meant 'a place or land' and so this was a land of service, so it was named Sevagram. My quick response to that explanation was 'You made a big mistake.' You should have named this place Kholagram."

"What does that mean?" I said.

"Khola means pumpkin, so I very boldly told him this should be called a land of pumpkins." We laughed. Head thrown back, wide grins.

I can just see it. Seven-year-old Ela, chin jutted out, speaking her mind to the famous Mahatma Gandhi. The innocence of a child.

Our laughter slowly subsided. She became serious again. "But he did not laugh at this," said Ela. "Instead he asked, 'Why do you say that' and I told him, 'I have never seen so many pumpkins as are seen here. We get them to eat every single day.' He took this childish talk seriously, and in the prayer meeting that evening he spoke about diet. He said living simply did not mean having no variety in the diet. He spoke at length about the need for variety and chided those who were serving pumpkins daily. This got me into trouble as the team responsible for catering began to look for the person who had been carrying tales to Bapuji. But for me this story revealed two things about him. First, how carefully he listened to our childish talk. How many of us pay attention to our children when they talk about the million things that they may have been up to?"

"So, you were a talkative child, then." I said.

"That's what they tell me," she said. "Sita, my sister, said I was very talkative, and in one of the letters I received from Gandhiji, he asked me if I was still as talkative as I had been when I was there."

"This news surprises me, because you are so calm, and you speak so quietly. But I would imagine you found your present voice as a result of later events. I'm sorry. I interrupted you, please continue. You were talking about how carefully he listened to you."

"Yes, in addition to that, his prompt reaction to the story, to correct the situation immediately again shows his efficiency and dedication to little details. We often forget that it is in the details that we slip up. Take care of the details and everything else falls into place."

The principle of efficiency and economy of effort again.

"That's a wonderful story," I said. "This is the first time I've heard you call him Bapuji. How is that different from Gandhiji?"

"Bapu refers to a respected elder and children often refer to their grandfathers that way. Ji is a term of respect. So Bapuji is something a child would say to a respected grandfather."

"Sort of like the different between Grandfather Raymond and Papa," I said. "The interactions with your grandfather, the pumpkins, the letters, that's such a precious memory."

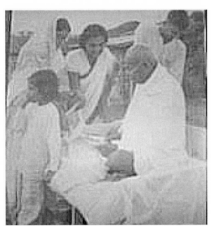

Seven year old Ela and Gandhi

"I have cherished this story since then," she said, "although I only began to understand the lessons much later. Today I see the importance of immediate action. For example, the civil service takes months to attend to a little issue that could be resolved in a much shorter time. If they were more efficient, they could prevent an unresolved issue from becoming a huge problem. Instead we continue to have disgruntled communities simply because of lack of efficiency and commitment to address issues immediately. I believe this is an important lesson for all of us."

"And you learned it at the knee of your Bapuji," I said.

She shook her head, yes. "I believe from my own life and experience, that lessons learnt at an early age remain, maybe subconsciously, but ultimately it is these lessons that provide one with the strength of character and wisdom needed when faced with the numerous challenges of life. Parents need to be conscious of what they are teaching their children and more especially what examples they are setting. We all learn much more from imitation than from lectures. We learn from observing and scrutinizing."

Sort of like showing rather than telling when writing a story.

"I think, at least in my own experience," she said, "children observe much more than adults do. A child can perceive the hidden things many others miss. They know when their parents feel anger, indifference, or they are irritated or dislike someone. Parents need to be attentive and extremely perceptive of the nonverbal messages they and the child are sending out."

We decided to take a short break for personal convenience. She disappeared down the hall and I walked over to the window. The sun was shining brightly, and the city in the distance was gleaming. Diamonds of light danced around the surface of the ocean. We began again.

"You were talking about how you learned to listen carefully to children through your grandfather's example," I said. "And you were also talking about your experiences with your grandfather. Is there more you would like to share on that topic?"

"Yes, it was 1946/47 at the peak of the negotiations and dealing with the delicate issue of Partition."

"And Partition was a brutal process," I said. "I have a friend whose family were Parsis and Zoroastrians. She said hundreds of thousands of people on both sides of the Indian/Pakistan border were killed."

"That is true," she said. "Men, women, children, and elderly people were killed on both sides because of the border dispute. It is always the weak who suffer in the aftermath of war."

"Unfortunately, we still see this everywhere in the world today." I shook my head. "Please continue."

"Even though his time was precious, my grandfather still found the time to speak to me on a daily basis for those few months. He gave us little children undivided attention when we were with him. When I returned to South Africa, he even corresponded with me, aged 7 years. How did he do this? He managed his time well and so he had time for every little thing that he felt was important."

Her principle of economy of effort in action.

"Good time management," she said, "can enable people to carry out their responsibilities ably, if they took it as an important aspect of life. Today's world can be a much better world if the people could be more other-centered than self-centered."

"Agreed," I said.

"Oh yes, I was very fortunate to have lived through experiencing two liberations. First was when we were in India. I was there in the little village where my maternal grandmother lived on August 15 when the Indian flag went up. I was the nearest relative to Gandhiji, so they asked me as a little child of 7 years to raise the flag. I vividly recall this, because it was such an experience to hoist the Indian flag and to feel that pride."

The crush of happy revelers. The shouts of joy, the jubilation and cheering in the crowd. So overwhelming and exciting for a little girl. The giddy rush, when she is scooped up off the ground and into the air, as if on a Ferris wheel.

"The second experience of liberation," she said, "was during the South African freedom. When we returned to South Africa, I used to tie a piece of handkerchief on a little stick and run around singing the freedom song. It was a cause for pride. Children still sing it today on August 15th.

Vijayi vishwa Tiranga pyara
Jhanda uncha rahe hamara
May my flag
always remain up high.

"Although we regarded South Africa as our country, we also felt pride that India was free at that time. The thing is, I spent about three months at Sevagram with my grandfather during that time and lived in his ashram under his supervision. That was a wonderful experience for me."

"I see the excitement on your face and hear it in your voice," I said. "The honor of raising the flag your grandfather fought for made an indelible impression," I said.

"'Twas exhilarating," she said.

I am sure this was the sea change moment that awakened the Gandhi Archetype within her. Ubuntu and Satyagraha were already flowing through her sweet little soul, and when her beloved Bapuji was murdered in cold blood at close range by a fellow Hindu, the seeds of activism were sown. Grandfather Gandhi said, "what a man thinks, he becomes." If this is true, then the thoughts and words conveyed to Ela throughout her developmental years, and her early awareness of her grandfather's love, attention, fame, and demise were powerful experiences in shaping the idealist Ela became.

Chapter 17

Education, Marriage, and Career

After a break for tea, we resumed the interview. "We were talking about your grandfather before our break," I said. "It seems to me that 1947 to 1949 was a pivotal period for you. You visited your grandfather in 1947 and he was assassinated in January of 1948. In a previous conversation you mentioned you waged Satyagraha against your parents for the privilege to go to public school in 1949. You were successful and started traditional education that year. Would you agree with that summary?"

"As far as you have described, yes," she said. "But there was another important event during that time. In January of 1949, tensions erupted between the Zulus and the Indians in Durban. Panic spread throughout the city. For several days there were violent attacks by Zulus on Indians and retaliation by Indians against the Zulus. It was dreadful. Eighty-seven Africans, 50 Indians, and five others died. Hundreds were injured. Well over a thousand houses, shops, and two factories were destroyed. The violence went all the way from Durban to Pietermaritzburg. Some called it a pogrom, or a massacre of one ethnic group against another."

"How frightening," I said.

I can see 9-year-old Ela, fear and confusion in her eyes.

"I recall my brother, Arun, came to school on that first day and picked me up and took me back to the Phoenix Settlement. Along the way, children were throwing stones at our car. 'Twas terrifying."

"Oh, my word," I said. I was astonished. I put the pen down and sat back for a moment.

What else has this dear woman suffered at the hands of cultural and racial controversy?

"I can see why you were terrified," I said.

"Yes," she said. "But to soothe my fears, people in the settlement told me this was God's place and so no one could touch it. Members of both the Zulu community and the Indian community worked together to protect the Settlement from harm during the riots. I saw in that a powerful message of equity, sacrifice, dignity and activism."

"These were powerful forces to navigate at such a tender age," I said.

Gandhi was a stretcher carrier for the Zulus during WWI. They repaid the favor decades later by protecting the Settlement.

"Yes, The Natal Indian Congress (NIC) worked all through the night that first night, even though the building they were in was put to flames. And the NIC moved thousands of Indians to refugee camps until the violence settled days later. In February, the African National Congress (ANC) and the South African Indian Congress (SAIC) met to plan a way to calm the situation. They created a joint statement calling for mutual understanding and goodwill."

"OK," I said. "I'm getting the different groups mixed up. The NIC represented the Indians just in KwaZulu Natal province, right?"

"Yes," she said.

"But the SAIC represented Indians across all of South Africa, correct?"

"Yes," she said.

"And the ANC represented indigenous Africans across the whole country?"

"That's right," she said.

"So, after the violence ended, you just picked up and went on about your business of going to school with this kind of hatred and animosity swirling around you," I said. "At age nine?"

"There was nothing to do but be patient and hope the different organizations would agree upon solutions," she said.

Ela in Sewing Class
Second row, second child from the right.

"So, what did you do?" I said.

"I went back to school," she said.

So much for the happy school days of childhood.

"When I entered school, I was placed in standard (grade) 3. In standard 4, I received a double promotion to standard 6. In standard 6, I took the national exam. To everyone's surprise, I passed and then went to Durban Girl's High School. I had to take a bus from home to the train station at Grayville, about 2 ½-3 kilometers from the school, and then walk the rest of the way to High School. I studied English, history, geography, hygiene, health sciences and maths."

"Were you good at math?" I said. "It has never been my favorite subject."

"Maths were my favorite subject," she said. "And I excelled in English but hated history."

"Well that's ironic, given all the historical events you found yourself in."

This caused her to chuckle. It was mostly a silent chuckle from deep within, escaping as air through her nose rather than sound through her mouth.

"I was not fond of history," she said, "because of the abiding feeling among my family that the history taught in school was completely different from the history we experienced. I have learned that history is a very important subject because people need to understand their roots and the lessons history can impart."

"Let me show you a picture of my matriculating class," she said. She pushed herself up from her chair, stretched, and walked slowly over to a shelf of books. Pulling a large, thick book from its location, she returned and set the book in front of me.

Ela's Graduating Class

"What a fine-looking group of scholars," I said. "But this picture tells a powerful story. It's certainly not a melting pot of races. One black. One female. This took a lot of bravery, tenacity, and feistiness."

"Yes," she said. "The triple oppression of being black, female, and poor ruined many lives."

"I remember you talked about this last year," I said. "Let's come back to that. I want to know what you did next in school."

"After I finished my matric (high school)," she said, "my teachers encouraged me to pursue the field of medicine because I had received top marks in mathematics. If you score in mathematics, then the logical route is to go for medicine and so most of the girls in my school who had done well in maths studied medicine. But I couldn't see myself dissecting animals. When I was in matric, we had to dissect a guinea pig, and, oh, it was just so difficult for me, even to the point where I couldn't sleep the nights that they dissected the guinea pigs. I would take them lettuce and feed them every morning only to see them later, on that board all cut up. It was just terrible, so the principles I learned in childhood of respecting life turned me away from medicine."

"I can understand that completely," I said. "I'm not squeamish when it comes to my own health, but I can't stand to see someone I love suffering. So, what did you do next?"

"The next logical field for a woman with high marks such as mine was law and so I took a bachelor's degree in law. I completed the first degree of courses and was going for the second degree, but it was around that time that my husband received his banning orders."

"Wait, what?" I said. "You got married somewhere in there?"

"Yes," she smiled. Her grin was devilish.

"I fell in love with my husband, Mewalal Ramgobin, when I was still in school and about 17 years old," she said. "He was a neighbor and my brother's friend. But my mother was not happy about this for two reasons. First, she thought I was too young to really decide on who I would end up marrying. Second, she felt that we were not really compatible. He was about 8 years older than me, and he had left school and was not certain about what he wanted to do. I was quite ambitious and wanted to study further and be a lawyer."

Sounds about right for a 17-year-old girl with big dreams of starting a future of her own.

"Mewa was running a family retail business," she said. "When I graduated and went to university, he decided to join me and took up the courses that I had enrolled for. We were at university together."

"That sounds very romantic," I said.

"Yes, but my mum felt I should go to India and take a gap year. During that time, I could think whether I really wanted to marry Mewa. So, I agreed. I was then 19 years old. My brother Arun, with his wife and newly born son, was living in India and I was happy to visit them and spend some time with them as well as my aunts and uncles."

"Sounds like you enjoyed India on this second visit?" I said.

"Yes, I did, and I got to spend time on my aunt's ashram. She was a social worker. She took in neighboring orphaned and, sometimes, ostracized children and began teaching and providing them with skills to be able to lead an independent life themselves."

"Excuse me," I said. "Ostracized children?"

"Yes," she said. "Children of mixed race were treated as less than the orphans and so she took them in."

This is so hard to fathom. I cannot imagine ostracizing a child under any circumstances.

"The ashram grew from these little beginnings," Ela said, "to house a huge school, a clinic, art classes and various extramural activities. Her ashram was popular and well-respected. She could have taken on the role of a village elder, all powerful. Instead she chose to live in simplicity on a little pension that her father had provided for her. The lasting impression it had deep down in my mind was revealed when I chose to have my marriage in that little village and in later taking on Social Work as my own career."

So service was a family tradition.

"By December 1960, I was still certain that I wanted to marry Mewa, and so my mum, who had joined us in India, suggested we have the wedding in India since our relatives would also like to see him. Mewa agreed to come to India. We had a beautiful wedding in the little village where my aunt had her ashram. We married in simplicity according to Gandhian ideals. All the villagers came to the wedding and my relatives too. It was a beautiful spirit. We stayed in India for a month and then returned home by ship, 21 days travel."

"I remember seeing the movie, Gandhi, with Ben Kingsley playing your grandfather," I said. "He and your grandmother, Kasturba, did a little re-enactment of their marriage vows. It was very sweet and simple."

"Yes, Mewa and I had our differences but, on the whole, we were happy, and people used to think we were an ideal couple because we were both involved in political work and complemented each other in the work. We lived at Phoenix Settlement with my mother. We had a fairly close relationship with Mewa's family as well and they would often visit. His mother would come and stay with us."

"And did you continue your studies?" I asked.

"I tried. But in 1950 the apartheid government created the Suppression of Communism Act. They defined communism as any act against the government. And they decreed that all schools and universities were to teach in the Afrikaans language, the language of the oppressor."

"Yes," I said. "You explained that to me last year. You were talking about the murder of the school children in Soweto."

"Yes," she said. "My husband had received his first banning orders, which prevented him from attending university."

Banning orders? I need to circle back to this topic. I jotted a note to myself.

"The University of Kwa Zulu Natal (UKZN) didn't have classes for non-white people during the day. Mewa was banned and could not be out at night, so he could not drive me. That meant I would have to walk to University by myself at night. This was just not safe, especially for a woman of color, and so I decided not to attend UKZN. But to study through correspondence meant I would have to learn Afrikaans, which I hadn't done. I had taken Latin as my second language in high school because, at the time in history, we opposed learning the language of the oppressor. I had an aversion to learning it."

"Do you know any Afrikaans now?" I said.

"Some, yes, I see it differently now. I have a lot of Afrikaner friends and I don't have the same aversion anymore. But as a result,

I didn't pursue a second degree. 'Twas only a few years later that I decided to pursue social work. I had one baby at that time, and I saw an ad in the newspaper for a voluntary post at the child welfare society and I said, 'This sounds very good, let me try.' My mother and husband tried to dissuade me. They said, 'Well, you know, you will hardly get anything for it,' but I didn't want to work for the money. I wanted to do something, and so I volunteered there for a whole year. The following year I took social work training."

I understand the dilemma. Countless young, working mothers went through my program at the university. It was always a struggle.

"So, the first year, I wasn't even a qualified social worker. I was getting to know what this field is all about and I found it very interesting. Just the kind of work that I would like to do. While I was working, I completed my social work degree through correspondence at the University of South Africa (UNISA). For social work, you didn't have to learn Afrikaans, only for the law degree. For social work, they credited me for a number of subjects I had already taken, which applied to my Honors degree, which is a two-year program. That was the end of my studies in Social Science. I later tried to complete my qualifications for a law degree, but there were too many intervening factors."

"More babies, for one, and apartheid for another," I said.

"Yes, for me, social work was also a huge battle because the emphasis on social work in this country was on case work. This caused a conflict. My co-workers and I were given a glimpse into the lives of non-Indians through this work, and this was not permitted under Apartheid."

"Yes," I said. "I recall the story about the Afrikaner who was afraid he would take out his wife's eyes."

She nodded. Her eyes were upward and to the left, as if seeing an old movie in her head. "Working across cultures was not permitted, and so some members of the social work organization were banned, and I was banned. The government did not want the organization to exist. We were all intimidated in various ways such as being questioned about our activities; pressure being applied on our employers to control our activities and so on. The second problem I had is that we worked on a case work basis, which means you look at the individual's problem. Instead, we needed to work on change within the community and on preventive work."

"I can see how community work rather than casework would be more consistent with the philosophy and lifestyle you were raised in," I said.

"Yes, that is one of the things I changed for myself and for the students that used to come to our office as interns."

Be the change you want to see in the world. A living application of one of Gandhi's most famous sayings.

"We would teach them that prevention is very important," she said. "For me it was a political work and we reached out to communities and helped them organize themselves. Causes of problems in the majority of cases were embedded in the economic system where poverty is entrenched. This means struggling with the system, and even mobilizing communities to take up the issues themselves. Segregation of services was mandatory, and I broke this rule and worked with people of all races. For this, I was banned for a short period. After my banning orders were lifted, my colleagues and I formed a group called the Concerned Social Workers Association (CSWA)."

"That is amazing," I said. "It is difficult enough to be a working mother, but to do so while under a microscope, and in peril as well, that took so much courage."

"Yes," she said. "But not to do so was not an option."

This being mid-afternoon, we agreed it was a good time to take a break.

"May I have lunch now?" Ela said.

Holy cow! I have been torturing her. I could listen for hours but give the poor woman a break.

"Absolutely," I said. "We can pick this back up whenever you are ready.

Chapter 18

Triple Oppression

We resumed the interview around 2:30. "Before the break," I said, "you were describing the early years of your career. You were working as a social worker and had one child. Would you pick it up from there?"

"Of course, in 1960 we were living in Durban. At that time, all Zulu and Indian political organizations were banned, and so we were forced underground. Many of our community leaders were in hiding. We used to have the NIC branch meetings in our house. It was a very small branch, but we had to be very careful because police and security forces were all over. We engaged in various community actions."

"Such as…" I said.

"I remember a three-day strike was called to halt the activity in the town. We would create fliers at our flat. The fliers urged people to stay at home, effectively on strike. Then we walked down the streets pushing fliers under people's doors."

I see Ela and a colleague, dressed in trench coats, backs to the corners of buildings, one as a lookout, the other slipping fliers through mail slots and under doors. But then again, I may have seen too much U.S. TV.

"The newspapers downplayed the strike," she said, "but it was in fact quite successful in bringing much of the activity in town to a standstill. It was dangerous to have meetings at our flat. Sometimes branch members would come in disguise. They would report the thoughts and actions of the other political organizations. We were part of the Congress Alliance and so carefully watched what they were doing."

"What was the Congress Alliance?" I said.

"It was an anti-apartheid coalition across South Africa led by the ANC."

"Very dangerous business," I said.

"Yes. We used to hide young men who were going into umKhonto we Sizwe or take messages for them to different locations. Very dangerous. But in 1961, I was ill with jaundice and completely bedridden for three months. We moved back to Phoenix and my mum took care of me. We stayed there until 1975, but we lost track of some of the underground members. In 1963, quite a few of them were arrested and imprisoned. In 1963, my husband was elected president of the SRC."

"So, the jaundice was a blessing in disguise," I said. "You mentioned to me earlier that all your children were born at the Phoenix Settlement with your mother's help."

"Yes, I completed my degree in 1963, the same year I had my first son, Kidar. Mewa completed his in 1964, the same year I had my second son, Kush. In 1965, I started work at the Durban Indian Child Welfare Society. At the same time, I went to UNISA, graduated in 1968, and had my first daughter that June. I returned to work after four months but was posted to a different township. We were the first welfare organization providing services in this township. It was very challenging. I learned a lot about community organizing and building local structures. However, in 1970, I was pregnant and this time with twins, so I could not return to work."

Well, maybe you slowed, but if I know anything about you, Ela, you did not stop.

"During that time," she said, "we decided to provide a minimal medical service for the community in the old Press building."

I was right! Slowed but didn't stop.

"Three of the Settlement's trustees were doctors," she said, "and they offered free services. We opened the clinic on Wednesdays and Sundays. They each worked for 3 hours a week. I worked as a doctor's assistant dispensing medicines under their guidance and helping with any nursing assistance that may have been needed. So,

I was twice a week at the clinic. It became such a success that we employed a nurse aid in 1964 to run the clinic. By 1965 it was open 6 days a week. We offered health care, a lecture series on Gandhiji, and we planned to build a museum library. Then, from 1965 to 1970, my husband was banned."

Next opportunity, I need to ask her about being banned.

"During this time in 1968," she said, "I was invited to address a meeting in Merebank, an Indian township in the south of Durban. The sports organizations held a meeting calling for boycott of racist sports. Many sports leaders addressed the meeting as well. We all stressed the fact that we cannot have normal sporting activities in a society where there was so much of discrimination. They tried to woo us by scrapping some of the segregation in sports. But this was a tactic and we called on the people not to fall prey. We said South African sports people must suffer the international isolation until South Africa is free."

"And you gave this address the same year you had your daughter," I said, "with two preschool age sons at home?"

"Yes." She waved the back of her hand in the air as if to say, "Of course. No big deal."

"After the meeting, when I was about to leave," Ela said, "I realized that someone had punctured all four of the tires of my car. Fortunately, there were many people still around and they helped me to get the tires fixed and I was able to travel home. It was a scary experience. But we were not prepared to be intimidated. We continued with the campaign."

We were not prepared to be intimidated. Can you prepare for intimidation? Remarkable.

"You mentioned to me the concept of bannings before our break," I said. "You said that they interfered with your ability to get a higher degree and to go about your work. Would you expand on this for me?"

"Bannings were a tool the apartheid government used to control us. If we engaged in any activity to improve things for non-whites, or we got involved in the lives of non-whites, this could result in a banning. If you are banned, then you are not allowed to communicate with more than one person at any time unless you are at home. A harsher version of this is house arrest. My husband and I were both banned, and we had to acquire special permission to be able to communicate with each other because two banned persons could not speak to one another other."

What a harsh ruling. To live with one's spouse but be banned from speaking to him or her?

"We were not allowed to have any visitors in the home as well," Ela said. "We could not leave the area. We were not permitted to attend social gatherings or meetings of any kind. But activities continued on the Settlement. We organized camps for students including those from the theological seminary. Speakers shared Gandhi's ideas. University students came to participate in political discussions. Students from the medical school came and provided services at the clinic. Some of these people are now Ministers in our democratic government."

So much activity under such restrictions.

"In 1970 my husband launched the Committee for Clemency for Political Prisoners. This later became the Release Mandela Committee. In 1971, an ad hoc committee to revive the Natal Indian Congress was formed. My husband was Chairman of the committee. He worked with a number of people from various areas of Natal. The government was trying to divide the Indians and the Blacks by offering minimal status in the government. We saw through this, though. They also began to move people into townships and rural areas and enforce segregation."

I feel the tension rising in her descriptions of events. As if a groundswell were building. It's hard not to get caught up in what she is saying, to remain focused on the interview, not the interviewee.

"By this time, in 1971, the government was starting to lose legitimacy within the international community. We did not want to be pawns in the hands of the apartheid government. That is why we revived the Natal Indian Congress to oppose these dummy government structures. And we engaged in many forms of activism.

We helped University students set up a benefit society for workers to pay for funeral expenses, medical aid schemes, boycotts of products created through unfair practices, and wage equity. Our boycotts were usually successful."

"And was Mewa working beside you in all of this? Such a challenge," I said.

"My husband was served with a second banning," she said, "and this time also house arrest orders for 5 years. NIC was launched on 25th June 1971. He was chairman and I was elected as the vice president. The conference was held at the Phoenix Settlement. My husband had to close his offices in Durban and open offices in Verulam as he was no longer allowed to travel to Durban because of the banning. After the launch of the NIC, we continued with political campaigns opposing the government's dispensations and intimidation tactics. In 1973, I was slapped with a banning and house arrest order."

Note to self. This is the third time she has mentioned house arrest. Something else I need to circle back around to.

"This was all so stressful. Did it take a toll on your marriage? So much activity," I said.

"Yes," Ela said. "It did. Life was difficult and yet very fulfilling to be at the Settlement and to work on some of the projects there. My husband was very happy working on getting the clinic started and setting up the museum and a library. He was an insurance broker. Two years after our house arrest orders in 1975, we decided to move to Verulam, a small town near Phoenix. This would offer better facilities for the children both in terms of schooling and in terms of their recreation. My mum was persuaded to come with us, after I agreed to take her back to Phoenix at least two or three times a week. Mewa would go frequently to oversee the work there and I gave voluntary service to the clinic and my mum would go with either of us as frequently as she wished to."

"Nice to have a third pair of hands with the children, I am sure," I said. She nodded, but she did not smile.

"During this time," she said, "it seemed that Mewa and I were slowly drifting apart. At the beginning, he was very supportive of all the work that I was doing, but slowly he began to drift away and show irritation and disregard for my work. I felt that it was just a passing phase and did not react."

I want to say something conciliatory, but I guess silence is better. He was under pressure as well.

"There was massive repression in the country," she said, "and my husband and several others were arrested and held in prison for about a week but were released on a technicality. Upon their release it was agreed they would go in to hiding. The new Apartheid parliament was about to inaugurate three separate segregated houses for the three races. These included Whites, Indians, and Coloureds, but excluded the African people. They sought refuge in the British Embassy on inauguration day."

To have to seek refuge in an embassy. The tension and fear must have been unbearable. But clever to tarnish the inauguration.

"This happened," Ela said, "and it was really a stroke of ingenuity because it captured the headlines all over the world. They stayed in the consulate for some weeks. Three came out but were immediately arrested and imprisoned with others from around the country, all of them accused of treason. A lengthy trial followed and at the end they were all found not guilty. We all passed through this harrowing period trying to keep our families, our jobs and taking care of the needs of those in detention. They, too, suffered the difficult prison conditions but came out strong. This all happened in the latter part of the 1980s."

Note to self. Ask how we jumped from '75 to the late '80s. What happened?

"It was during this time I realized that my husband was seeing someone else. This led to tensions in our home, and the children, who were all teenagers by then, felt that it was time we separated."

Amazing kids.

"Verulam was a small town," she said, "and virtually everyone knew what was happening. Mewa moved out and into a flat nearby. I was devastated at the time and felt I needed a change from child welfare work to something less stressful, and so I took a full-time position at the Career Information Centre in Durban and then decided to move into a small flat I could maintain myself. I had spoken to the children and they all accepted that this would be in our best interest. We could then become more self-reliant and not dependent on my husband who had to pay the bond on the house, which was quite big and costly. Three of my children moved with me. Two opted to stay on in Verulam, in our previous house."

The dissolution of any family unit is stressful. It couldn't have been easy.

"I then sought a divorce," said Ela, "and that was quite easily finalised as I did not ask for anything from my husband and he did not oppose it. The children, too, were all beginning to be self-sufficient. My husband officially began living with the woman he had fallen in love with and had a son with her. Some years later he married her."

Not sure I would have been so peaceable.

"My husband remained involved in political work," she said. "He was a good orator and organiser. We both belonged to the same organisations and continued to work together. He was elected into the first democratic parliament and served four terms in parliament before retiring."

I need a moment to process this. Best to be silent and let her continue.

"I have had only one man in my life," said Ela, "and after him, I have never thought of another marriage or a relationship. I still cherish the good years that we spent together and supported each other in all the work that we did. Perhaps one takes a relationship for granted and doesn't work at maintaining it, or there could be other reasons. Whatever they were, he started another relationship and that brought to an end our marriage. Today it is no big issue as divorces are a common occurrence, but for me it was not a common occurrence."

"Nor would it be for me," I said. "But you don't seem bitter. In fact, I think it spurred you on to continue your work on women's issues."

"Yes, Nelson Mandela said that freedom cannot be achieved unless women have been emancipated from all forms of oppression. And Gandhiji said that poverty is the worst form of violence. So, I became very much involved in the gender struggle in South Africa because women suffered a triple oppression."

"You talked briefly about this in your Atlanta presentation," I said. "But refresh my memory."

"We suffered," she said, "because we were poor, we were women, and we were black. And so, it was a triple oppression. Women all along suffered because they were the poorest in terms of wages and possessions. They were right at the bottom, and that was the first thing. You shared the race and black oppression with men and women, but the gender oppression put us right at the bottom of the scale. Gandhiji said poverty is the worst form of violence."

She seems to be getting a second wind.

"Women always had to do double duty," she said. "Women go to work and then come home and continue to work at home, looking after the children, looking after the husband, and there was no relief. Secondly, there were many laws that discriminated against women, such as succession laws and ownership laws. It was worse for African women. But women elect the men, so education and empowerment are needed. Women have a lot of leadership qualities but the culture at that time didn't encourage assertiveness and self-confidence. Women didn't project themselves as men did. In South Africa there were many men who knew very little, but they were able to articulate and so they became leaders. At the same time there were women who knew a lot but kept it to themselves."

Same everywhere around the world.

"This was not right, so we tried to empower women, bring them together, give them self-confidence, let them stand up for their rights within the sheltered grouping of women, and so we formed a women's organization that was very powerful. From the early days, women marched, and they amazed the men in the way they were able to organize."

We were interrupted by a phone call. I took the opportunity to stand and walk a bit. She returned and resumed her comments.

"My mother comes from a very powerful family. Her uncle was a confidant and general advisor to Gandhiji. And then my mother's family, my aunt and all the others were freedom fighters as well, participating in the freedom struggle. They were activists during the time of India's independence. It was an organized marriage between my mum and dad. For her first trip out of India as a young lady, she came to South Africa alone, where there were no relatives. She took the plunge and came here, and she became an equal partner to my father, learning everything about the printing press and assisting my father in running it. Although she was never imprisoned or anything like that, she would help my dad whenever there was any political activity."

She definitely has a second wind.

"My mother also told me stories, about powerful women and so they were my role models. She told me stories of women like Lakshmi Bai, the Queen of Jhansi, who was one of the leading figures of the rebellion in India in 1857, leading skirmishes against multiple intruders. She told me about powerful women, freedom fighters, governors, and organization presidents. And then, of course, there was my aunt, whose picture I always keep. Hearing about strong women certainly had an effect on my life. I believe children need stories about strong heroes, not stories about un-realistic fantasies."

"It is said behind every great man, there is a great woman," I said. "I would wager to say that behind every great woman, there is a great mother."

"'Twas that way in my case," she said.

The role of women in the betterment of humanity has always been undervalued, under-described, and underappreciated.

"In current society," Ela said, "when people talk about women's rights, there is emphasis on getting into previously male-dominated jobs or higher positions. But we cannot confuse jobs with roles. Roles come from childhood, the way we bring up our children. We teach our children that this is what a woman is supposed to do, and this is what a man is supposed to do. All the jobs of taking care of children, sick people, and old people belong to the women."

So true.

"And we accepted this; we are brought up believing it. My view is that our responsibility is everybody's responsibility, the male and the female, and that if a person needs care, then both have to do it together. If there are sick people in the home, if there are people living with disabilities, we have a joint responsibility to take care of them, and if we accept that, then women would be able to use their power. Equality in responsibilities and in jobs means that you share the jobs and the roles."

"I like this emphasis on roles," I said. "That's not a perspective you often hear. You hear conversations of pay equity and of how many corporations don't have female CEOs. It's always equity in the direction of aligning women with men. But what about aligning men with women? Where are the conversations about household workload equity or of how many men don't take their daughters to ballet class?"

"Children today do not receive the same amount of attention as they used to," said Ela, "Parents end up in old age homes, the sick end up in hospices. If we took joint responsibility for the roles needed in a family, we would be able to plan better. This applies to society as well. Employers need to recognize that men and women have children. Men and women need facilities for these children. Men and women need time off to fetch the children from schools. This should not be available only to people in industry and university but to the domestic workers as well. What about their children? Ordinary people doing ordinary jobs also need help. Society needs to organize itself so that everybody is taken care of."

She is so right.

"My grandfather was once asked why he was opposed to machinery," she said. "He said he would like to live in a village where there were not so many implements. He said that he was not opposed to anything that one invents to makes life easier, but he was opposed to a machine that was going to replace a person. Everybody should have the right to have some form of employment. He thought the differentiation and categorization of people in terms of where they live, what they wear, what they eat, the color of their skin, or their gender are all a means to divide society."

Agreed.

"In seeking independence or freedom, we must not discard the good attributes we have within ourselves and ape the attributes of the oppressors. This is the tragedy. We don't want to lose all the good that different roles bring to the world. Otherwise we just end up adopting the attitudes and teachings of the oppressors. Gandhiji believed that we should guard the feminine spirit of compassion, caring, loving and if a man chooses those roles, so be it."

At this point, Ela's phone rang.

Saved by the bell. I have tortured her again.

Ela went to the hallway to answer the phone. I did not actively listen, but I did overhear. If you don't want to see something, close your eyes. If you don't want to feel something, don't touch it. If you don't want to taste something, don't put it in your mouth. But hearing does not give us the same option. It is there 24/7/365. So, I overheard her conversation. The Dalai Lama was coming to Durban to receive an International Peace Award from the Gandhi Development Trust. If we had just waited a month for this trip, we would have had the opportunity to meet him personally.

"Mandela, Tutu, the Pope. Who don't you know?" I said when she returned.

"I don't know Oprah," she said.

Chapter 19

A Crazy Cab Ride

"Are you getting anything good for your book," Gwen asked. We were having breakfast the next morning at the hotel.

"And how," I said. "Ela will have lots of stories to pick from for a collection."

Another incredible smorgasbord of international options. Eggs made in every way imaginable. Meat dishes from chicken, beef, lamb, and seafood to the more exotic water buffalo. Rice, steaming potatoes, and crusty breads, hands down a favorite comfort food worldwide.

"Mmm," said Gwen.

"Did you see all the cheese, juice, and coffee options?" said Sue.

"Too much for the imagination," I said. "I'm opting for my usual spinach, mushroom, and cheese omelet."

We carried our laden plates to one of the tables near the windows and set them down, watching the bustle of the new business day outside. The cacophony of cars, buses, the ding-ding of bicycle bells, shouts, and conversation of the city at morning was damped by the thick panes of glass. Like watching a movie with the sound off.

"Are you ready for your presentation?" I said to Sue. We were addressing members of the International Education Association of South Africa-IEASA. Attendees were expected from around the continent.

"I have another meeting to go to first," said Gwen. "Y'all go ahead and I'll join you at the conference later."

"That's fine," I said. "We'll take a cab and see you there."

"Just watch out for the taxi wars," she said.

"What?" I turned to her sharply.

"It's in the paper," she said.

"Details, details," I said.

"Who knows what's going on," she said. "The paper said turf wars have been happening for decades, but I don't know what the strike is about."

First the teachers, now the taxi drivers.

"Nobody else looks concerned," Sue said. "But we can check at the concierge desk."

"I feel safe," I said. "After all, this is almost a decade after apartheid, and Papa Mandela is doing a great job leading the country to freedom and peace. I'll admit it took me a while to get over the barbed wires atop all the homes and buildings and hired guards stationed on most streets, but that just comes with the territory when you go outside the U.S., right?"

"It'll be fine," Sue said. We walked to the desk and expressed our concerns.

"Oh, no, ma'am," the concierge said. "There should be no problem at all."

But the newspapers told a different story. Apparently, a taxi strike was underway. Small battles were breaking out surrounding the rights of one driver over the rights of another to park in a certain location or to pick up certain guests.

As fate would have it, a White Afrikaner driver, who was next in the taxi line to receive a paying customer, picked us up to transport us to the conference. He opened the door of a large, white, multi-seat van. He was tall, strong, perhaps in his 50s, with almost white, blonde hair. He was rugged looking, like he belonged on an emergency rescue crew in the mountains somewhere. We shrugged off concerns surrounding the potential for violence.

Everything's fine. He speaks English so there won't be any confusion. And he can explain the strike to us.

I was wrong.

"Where to, ma'am," said the driver.

"We're going to the IEASA conference," I said.

"Sure, no problem," he said.

As he pulled out of the parking space, a black sedan drove by and our driver violently pounded the car horn. He let out a string of expletives that would have made a longshoreman blush.

That's bizarre. Sue and I looked at one another, eyes wide. And that's when I lit the fuse.

Curiosity killed the cat, they say.

"We read in the newspaper that there is a taxi strike going on," I said. "We were afraid we wouldn't find a taxi to the conference. Whaatt's gooiinng onnn?"

I didn't actually say it that way, but when I relive the experience, I always hear myself saying it in slow motion.

"What's going on?" he said. "What's going on is the #%*$ (racial slur) drivers are taking our work. They are pushing us out. They think they own everything now. Them and their music."

The van swerved close to the curb. He corrected the course just in the nick of time.

"They think we don't know what they are trying to say," he said. "They sing about the Boers. They say they are going to make sure the Boers get what is coming to them. But we'll see who gets what's coming to him. I used to have a high position in the secret forces, and I know many ways to 'take care of' the #%*$ (racial slur) drivers." He made air quotes with the fingers of his left hand, the right holding and releasing, holding and releasing the steering wheel.

Oh, geez. Is he like the guy Ela spoke of who could pull out his enemy's eyeballs?

"See this?" he said. He pulled a gun out from under his seat and waved it around. "This is all we need," he said. "Don't worry. I have everything under control."

Oh, crikey. Everything but yourself. Better hold our tongues here.

Sue and I stared at each other, doing our best to maintain an expressionless face, reading a similar message in one another's eyes.

"They are all just cheating, stealing low life," he said. "We can wait, though. Things are about to explode." This, as he swerved into oncoming traffic, once again correcting course in time to avert disaster. His face became redder with each declaration. The blaring of horns erupting, then subsiding.

"Oh, ho, ho, ho," he said with a sinister chuckle. "We are just waiting. Retaliation will be ours. We'll put those #%*$ (racial slurs) back where they belong, and they won't rise up when we're done next time." He spoke "won't rise up" in a growl, teeth clenched.

Is he saying what I think he's saying?

"And they better not think the police are going to save them. We know the police. We'll even the score before the police show up." Spittle sprayed from his mouth.

"They pushed us out once," he said, "but we will push back harder. Nobody takes from us forever." He pounded the steering wheel with his open hand. "It's our God-given right!"

The driver continued his rant, sharing inflammatory interpretations of the local headlines. His not-so-thinly veiled threats suggested he was just waiting for the first opportunity to even some score. He drove at a breakneck speed, drifting at the curves, and cursing at his and other vehicles. He was clearly on a mission that had little or nothing to do with his passengers in the back seat.

Praise the Universe, we finally arrived at the conference site. We paid him and gave him a better tip than he deserved. Thank goodness for Sue's laid-back, calm demeanor. But we were both clearly shaken.

"Here is my card," he said. He thrust it toward me, and I visibly jumped. "Call me when you need to come back from your meetings," he said. "You don't want to get into any taxis with a #%*$ (racial slur)."

"Thank you," I said. *Nor do I want to get back into a van with you.*

"Come on," said Sue. She grabbed the arm of my suit jacket and pulled me toward the conference venue doors. The driver, still standing and watching us leave, started circling around his van, stamping his feet, continuing his rant, waving his gun.

"Oh, good Lord," I said once we were safely inside. "That was intense."

This is just not right.

"I've been in a half a dozen taxis here," I said, "all driven by other races, and I've never felt intimidated like this. None of the other drivers were anything but cordial. No one from the other race groups showed us anything but their personal sense of dignity."

"He was really sick," Sue said. "The Black women who helped us with our rooms were skilled and graceful; the Coloured women at the school were smart, cordial and gracious; the Indian participants in our workshops have all been gentle and well-spoken."

"Is that what's really going on here?" I said. "Is there that much thinly veiled anger and animosity seething below the surface?"

I wanted to cry, but hundreds of other conference goers were milling around.

"Oh, thank goodness," said Sue. She spotted Lavern, who was walking toward us. A friendly face. The voice of calmness and composure. We both grabbed onto him, hoping some of his self-control would rub off.

The conference went well. Needless to say, we returned by a different cab, and our driver could not have been more helpful and courteous.

I've read about it. I've seen it on TV and in the movies. The murder of Steve Biko. The slaughter of innocent children. But watching others' fear and experiencing it yourself are two different things. And does loss of privilege and status always turn people in the direction of this crazy racist driver? I need to ask Ela about it. Maybe she can help me see a broader perspective.

Chapter 20

House Arrest

The morning after the IEASA conference, I prepared to head for my final interview with Ela. Notebooks, pens, recorders, and cassettes were once again crammed into my work bag. I stepped outside the hotel lobby and walked toward the first available taxi in the line. A visceral response from the previous day's taxi ride caused me to turn around, pretending I forgot something.

That's ridiculous, Susan. Surely that was a rare event. Put on your big girl pants.

The next driver was small in stature, drove a mid-sized sedan rather than a big van, and met me with a smile.

I outweigh him by quite a few pounds. If nothing else, I could sit on him if things go south.

"Hello, Ma'am," he said. His voice was quiet, his actions subdued.

A Black African of mixed race. Probably Zulu and Indian, maybe a white ancestor thrown in there somewhere.

"Where shall I take you, Ma'am?"

I gave him Ela's address.

"Are you here on business?" he said.

I gave a brief version of my purpose.

"Ah, an educator," he said. "I, too, am an educator. I have my master's degree. But it has been difficult to find work in schools nearby my home, and for now, driving pays more. Education pays those of my race less well. But we are a changing country. Things will get better."

No rant. No spittle. No pounding. Just a reasoned comment. What a contrast. Yesterday's driver was educated in violence and feels cheated of his due. Today's driver is educated in service, slightly defensive, but feels appreciative of his options.

We arrived at Ela's.

"Here is my business card, Ma'am," the driver said. "If you need a ride back, my number is at the bottom." He pointed to it.

"Thank you," I said. I didn't jump. I didn't even flinch. There was no fear, only cordial interaction.

"It won't be until mid-afternoon," I said. "If my colleague doesn't pick me up, I'll call you."

"Pleasure," he said, nodding to me.

I knocked on Ela's door. "Welcome again," she said. "Please come in. There's the table. Let me move these papers out of your way. What is our agenda for the day?" She gathered her papers together with a brushing motion of her hand.

I began setting up the equipment. "There are two things that came up during our conversation yesterday," I said. "I want to examine those, but first, may I tell you about an experience I had yesterday? It was quite unsettling."

"Please," she said. She motioned me to sit. "Tea?"

"Yes," I said. "Thank you." I gratefully accepted her offer. I described the disturbing taxi ride.

"We spoke some of this previously," said Ela. "The White Afrikaners felt that they were the privileged race and it was hammered into them from early childhood that the Black people were there to do their work and were not at the same level as them. They were taught this idea of a worthier race throughout their lives. They would be harsh with people who wanted to bring about changes. That is understandable, but how do you explain a Black person becoming as harsh or worse than the white? When Black people received a change in status, some took on the brutality of the white men. How do you explain this? What was in it for them?"

"So, this is the source of the turf war, then," I said. "Both sides still struggling for a stronghold?"

"Yes," she said. "In fact, it was a Black policeman who came to our house that day while we were under house arrest."

"That folds nicely into the next question I want to ask. But can we continue here for a moment? What do you think accounts for the first taxi driver's actions?"

"It is the same old struggle for resources. If you had resources and lost them, you feel the lack. If you never had resources and want them, you feel the lack. Lack easily becomes defensiveness, and defensiveness can become greed. Defensiveness is just a more tolerable version of greed as it places the blame on the other person. In either case, the aggrieved party needs to take responsibility for his own actions."

Her principle of personal responsibility.

"Wow, Ela," I said. "That is really profound. I'd never thought of defensiveness as a form of greed based on a sense of lack, or that defensiveness involves avoidance of personal responsibility."

"Well, that is what I was taught, and it is what I believe," she said.

"But defensiveness feels less dangerous," I said.

"Yes, unless it becomes insidious and festers. Then it becomes greed, and then violence. And so, we must help people face themselves when they are defensive. This may prevent worse problems from arising."

I love this thought. I know so many people who are defensive. I need to imagine a kinder way of dealing with them, of helping them deal with the root cause of their defensiveness; the feeling of lack. And I need to watch for defensiveness in myself. Call myself out first.

"That's really beautiful, Ela," I said. "If we could all do this, what a better world we would live in. You have given me something important to think about."

She nodded her head. Her eyes closed and opened with the nod.

"Back to our previous interview, there are two questions that came up. First, you mentioned the concept of house arrest a couple times, and then you were talking about 1975 and skipped to the end of the 80s. I feel there is a big chunk of missing information. Would you address those two topics, please?"

Ela stood up, poured more tea, and walked over to the windows. She adjusted the blinds as the sun was rising in the late-morning hours. Then she came to the table and sat down.

"To refresh your memory," I said, "you briefly touched on your house arrest and its influence on your children in your Atlanta presentation, and the other day you mentioned that you moved to Verulam in 1975. Can we start there?"

She nodded assent. She shifted in her seat, raising and lowering her knees, getting comfortable for a long discussion. She leaned forward, arms folded, resting on the table.

"There were actually three types of orders," she said. "The first was a banishment from participating in the activities of organizations. The second was a stricter banishment from any interactions with groups of any kind. The third was a house arrest. I wasn't the only one who was house arrested and banned," she said. "There were many people in South Africa who suffered house arrest and banning orders. Whites as well as Blacks, Coloureds, and Indians were at risk. Many people were arrested and imprisoned for 90 days or more because of their political activities. It was really difficult."

Humans invent all sorts of ways of separating themselves from one another. Get a church together and before you know it, they have split into two factions. Get a group of teens together, and before you know it, you have cliques. It's a sad commentary on the human condition.

"The regime tried to kill us and my family," said Ela. "For example, there was the incident of a parcel bomb that was sent to my husband's office in 1973. This was the first of its kind at the time. He was lucky to escape with his life. And years later, they arrested my children, but they were released right away."

Shocking. So, she means literally, the regime tried to kill them.

She sat back in a more relaxed posture. Her eyes softened.

"At the time of my banning in 1973, I was just 33 years old. My children were just growing up. My twin daughters, Ashish and Arti, were three years old, and my oldest son, Kidar, was about to be 10. By the time the house arrest order was lifted in 1982, he was 19 years old. And the most formative years of his life were spent with us parents, who were both banned. Kush, born in 1964, was nine; Asha, born in 1968 was five."

"So, you had five children in 7 years? That's enough of a challenge."

She smiled. "My husband was also banned and house arrested as I was. House arrest restricted the hours you could be out of the house. If you needed anything during house arrest hours, you had to depend on a friend. You could go to work, but that was all."

"Yes," I said. I remember you described this in your Atlanta presentation. What other restrictions did you have?"

"I may have said this before," she said.

"That's OK," I said. "You can edit it out later."

"We couldn't communicate with people. We couldn't attend social functions, whether a family function or social activity—we couldn't attend. And the children grew up under those circumstances. So even today you will see those scars left on my children because of that banning order. You also see this on children of other banned people and house arrested people and those who suffered incarceration."

Reminds me of all the little children in Rwanda who suffered through genocide and the life of a refugee. My adopted son one of them. Why must the world be so cruel to children?

"But it was the price we felt we had to pay in order to win the freedom wanted in our country," she said. "And I didn't think it was a big price. There were people whose lives were taken by the Apartheid government; others were tortured and killed in detention. And when you compare yourself to that kind of incarceration, you think what you are undergoing is not that serious. This is what kept us going and gave us the spirits we had to continue."

"I am struggling to see that perspective," I said. "A friend of mine was in an abusive relationship. One day she was driving down the road and passed a prison van. She thought 'things could be worse. I could be in prison.' This is when she realized she had to get out. Just because someone else's life is worse, this does not diminish what you were suffering."

Different time, different circumstances. Let her talk.

"Yes," she said. "It did not diminish our suffering, but it gave us courage to continue the struggle." She stared out the window for a moment.

I wonder what terrible scene she is re-playing.

"During the time of emergency, a number of people were arrested. House arrest was difficult for my children because they didn't get all the things other children enjoyed like picnics and holidays. It was 15 years for my husband; my 8 ½ years of house arrest occurred during his banning. During that period, because he was banned, it was unsafe for me to go out."

"Please explain what you mean by a time of emergency," I said.

"If the government chose to declare a state of emergency," she said, "then they could impose stricter controls on those they felt were ungovernable. They used imprisonment, force, bannings, house arrests, and other acts of brutality. From the 50s to the beginning of the 90s, more than 2,000 people and organizations received banning orders. When you are banned you essentially are a non-person."

"Oh, my stars," I said. "So that is what was happening during the 1975 to late 80s period?"

"Yes," she said. "After my husband's arrest and then release along with two others, and before they went to the British Embassy, the Special Branch of the police came looking at my home for the three of them. The policeman said to me, 'You are the main one, and I can't believe you don't know where they are, and if you don't tell me where they are, you're going to find your husband torn into little bits!' My children were all awake at that time and heard. The kind of language he used was just horrible. There were lots of other people around who swore at them and tried to chase them off. But I told the police to come in to have a look. I said, 'He's not here and I have no idea where he is.' The policeman came in and searched the balcony but couldn't find my husband. He started getting very angry at me, thinking I was telling a lie. And so, I told him, 'Mr. Benjamin, let me ask you one question: Does your wife know where you are right now?" Ela chuckled, bending forward at the waist.

"He was absolutely stunned," she said, "and just put his head down and stormed out."

"Good," I said.

Hearing a soft word about his relationship to his own wife, he hung his head, and Ela won.

"After this," she said, "I was banned."

"Oh," I said. The weight of the experience sank in.

"Yes," Ela said. "For a long time, they ignored me, they laughed at me. When they couldn't ignore me, they harassed me, banned me, arrested me. But this just strengthened my resolve, especially when they turned to the use of foul language and intimidation. I knew I had won in that situation."

"Your grandfather said, 'First they ignore you, then they laugh at you, then they fight you, then you win.'"

"There was another time Mr. Benjamin came to our house at Phoenix Settlement," said Ela. "This was before we moved. At that time, I had an Alsatian dog who had alerted us that the police were at the door. The police wanted a typewriter to see if a document they thought was seditious was typed on that typewriter, but it was at Mewa's office. They wanted to take my husband to his office and get the typewriter, but I told them, 'We have a car and I'm prepared to take my husband there. You don't have to.' The police agreed but sent a couple officers with us to make sure we didn't go away somewhere else. I said, 'That's fine, but you can sit in the back.' The police got into the back seat, and then I opened the door to the car. I called my Alsatian. He was a very sweet and gentle dog, but they didn't know. He jumped into the front seat, then jumped over the guys in the back seat and on into the back of the van."

A huge, hairy dog with large ears and formidable fangs. I can picture it now. Long legs scrambling to the back seat, landing on the knees and chests of the police, ears flapping in their faces. Then hot breath, a lolling tongue, and large, sharp teeth between their heads when he made it to the back and turned around.

"This was comical and so I laughed and said, 'You can watch us, but my dog is watching you!' They were so terrified."

"And these actions led to your house arrest," I said.

"They contributed," she said. "As well as our underground activities. The day they brought me my house arrest order, my husband was already serving a banning order, and my son was having a birthday party. He was a little fellow, about to be 10. All the children ready to come to the party. When the person serving the orders came into my house, I was busy baking and getting things ready for the party and he said, 'We've brought banning orders for you and these are the conditions: you can't have any guests and I explained, 'We've got a party on the way.' But he said, 'You can't have a party' and I countered, 'Yes, I can because it's my son's party and he's not banned. He will have visitors, but I won't talk to them.' And so, I refused to obey the order. I said to myself, 'To hell with all these people. I'm not going to obey this order.' But after that we had to be careful."

"It must have been extremely difficult not to communicate with people," I said.

"I did break the orders several times," she said, "but I made sure there was nobody around because, when you break an order, the people around you are required to give evidence against you. That puts your friends into a difficult position because they don't want to betray you. But if they don't, they can be locked up and so you have a responsibility to protect them as well."

Not unlike Nazi Germany.

"That would be so difficult," I said. "Very hard to turn a friend or family member over to the police. But I am sure it was also difficult not to break such restrictive rules."

"Often it was difficult but the cause was bigger than all the anger and all the frustration."

The cause was bigger than all the anger and all the frustration. I cannot imagine trying to raise five active children under such restrictions, knowing at any moment you could receive an even stricter penalty. But this cause wasn't just about politics or ideologies. It was about survival.

"We felt that this was something that had to be done," she said. "Both my husband and I felt the people in prison were suffering more. They were hanged or gave up their lives for the struggle. So, the banning order was nothing. That's how we looked at it. We told ourselves and each other, 'We'll survive, we're going to continue with the struggle. There's no way they will imprison our spirit.'"

There's no way to imprison our spirit. Remarkable.

"And so, we had the birthday party. I just put the food out and stepped back. If I had sat with the children, they could have charged me, and I didn't want to antagonize them on the first day."

"And they couldn't have waited a couple hours for the party to end?" I said. "What difference would it have made? That was just plain meanness."

"Yes, I did the best I could to give my children as normal a family life as possible. Those in power tried to break the fabric of my family to force me into submission."

By threatening her family life and the safety of her children, they attempted to crush her. But it didn't work.

"Those are the kind of incidents that happened," Ela said. "Later we had to find ways of moving around under those circumstances. We were still actively fighting apartheid. We would make an appointment to meet friends on the street. Sometimes they would sit somewhere with us in the car, where we made sure nobody was watching and taking pictures. The police used to have a car parked just near our house and would watch who was coming and going.

Those banning orders were something else. The orders say that you are a threat to the State, but we were only trying to live our lives and improve conditions."

"Were there other requirements?" I said.

"Yes, every Saturday we had to go to the police station and sign our names to prove we hadn't skipped the country or anything like that. One Saturday I forgot to go to the police station and didn't remember it until Monday. But by that time, I had made friends with many of the policemen and so I went and asked, 'Let me just sign for Saturday if you don't mind' and the policeman on duty agreed, so I signed for Saturday on Monday." Ela laughed, a big laugh this time. Head back as if remembering a victory.

"They were all just human. Most of the police did not try to hurt us, but the Special Police, those were horrible characters. They tortured our people. They killed our people. They had no conscience, no compassion. They were really hardened guys."

"So that brings us to the late-70s," I said. "What happened after that?"

"In January of 1980," she said, "We were hit with a cholera epidemic.

A cholera epidemic? What next?

"My children were now ages 10 to 17. It was a very unsettling time. People were displaced. The Department of Health, Welfare, and Pensions advised local authorities to educate the public on being hygienic. But pure drinking water was unavailable in the slums and shanties. The government said it did not have the resources to provide water across the country. But they were able to arrange this in other towns. The government washed its hands of us and left it up to local authorities to handle. Things were particularly hard in the Black community because they were more susceptible to the disease and were less likely to have pure water than the Whites. Many of the cases in Inanda were related to pollution of the water. By the end of the first year, over 14,000 people had cholera in KZN and 50 died."

"It must have been horrifying, trying to keep your children safe from cholera while under house arrest," I said. "This would be a mother's worst nightmare."

"'Twas a difficult time," she said.

I wonder what else happened in the 80s.

"In 1987 I sought a divorce, and that was quite easily finalized as I did not ask for anything from my husband, and he did not oppose the divorce. The children were ages 17 to 24 and were all beginning to be self-sufficient."

I should know not to ask, "what next." The answer always makes me wish I hadn't.

Harassment, banishment, house arrest, cholera, and a divorce. The 1980s were unkind to Ela.

Chapter 21

Burning Down the House

After a morning's conversation about such difficult concepts as house arrest, cholera, and divorce, Ela and I took a break. I wandered once again around her apartment. There was her bust of Gandhi. There was the murderer's spoon. There were some of her awards. It felt as if I were seeing old friends.

"Let me know when you are ready to start again, Ela," I said. "I know I push you kind of hard. Remember, we can always stop when you need a break."

"I'm ready to start now," she said.

"Excellent. Then it looks to me as if we have covered most of the 80s. Now we are in the 90s. I know that was an exciting time because of Mandela's release from Pollsmoor Prison. You mentioned that in Atlanta. Do you have more you want to tell me about the 80s?"

"Perhaps some more detail," she said. "In order to do that I need to give a little background from the 70s."

"Start where you think is best," I said.

"As you know, we moved away from the Phoenix Settlement a couple years before I was house arrested. As a result, the land lay unused. During the 70s, unrest grew. To quell the unrest, the government took steps to ensure that most of the African people remained in their tribal homelands. Laws preventing them from moving into the cities were more stringently applied."

Banished from the cities?

"Homelands were consolidated," she said. This separated the tribes into independent, self-governed entities. Leadership was consolidated and imposed on the people. These so-called leaders repressed and victimized popular local leadership and any opposition to the homeland and apartheid governments."

Um. What? The response was to tell them to get out and leave us alone? Sort of like what we did to the native Americans. I guess my basket idea had a smidgen of merit after all.

"At the same time," Ela said, "the apartheid government tried to appease the Indian and the Coloured communities. I mentioned before that they tried to put Indians and Coloured people on a council, just to pacify them. In 1983, they offered us a tricameral, or three-chamber parliamentary system based on race. Members were to be elected by their respective race groups, but the white chamber would control the budget. This was not acceptable because the majority of people in the country, the African people, were left out of this government."

Difficult to imagine anyone thought this was acceptable.

"The 1984 House of Delegates attempted to have an election, but only 6% of the Indian population voted. People in the tribal homelands did not accept their independent status because it left them out of government altogether."

"OK," I said. "So, let me get this straight. The government's response to non-Whites was to send the tribal Africans packing, and to lump the Indians and Coloureds together in theory but give them no actual power, the country's budget being the power source?"

"Yes," she said. "They could then say, 'Well we gave them a voice.'"

What a sham. Paternalism in all its glory.

"Prior to this, around 1976, the South African Indian Council (SAIC) started to build housing for the Indian community. They purchased land from the huge sugar cane barons. They replaced the sugar fields with a massive low-cost housing scheme for the Indian community in the Phoenix Township. This land was adjacent to the sprawling Inanda area, an area the government had not designated for the use of any specific race group. Since the early 20th century the area was occupied by people of all races. That's how Mahatma Gandhi set up his settlement."

Not unlike the westward expansion of the late 19th to early 20th centuries in the U.S.

"Thus," she said, "the Phoenix Settlement was part of Inanda and not part of the Phoenix Township. There was an influx of African people from rural areas seeking jobs. They built their homes in Inanda and worked the land."

Confusing. Phoenix Settlement was in Inanda and primarily Black. Phoenix Township was adjacent and primarily Indian. I'm sensing things aren't going to go well with this situation.

"And so, there were problems?" I said.

"Yes, this is because the Inanda area was not serviced. Water, sanitation and schooling became a problem."

"Is that what people mean when they speak of informal housing?" I asked. "They are off the public grid? No services? And this resulted in the outbreak of cholera you mentioned."

"Yes," she said. "And typhoid."

Oh geez. What next? Wait. Don't ask. The answer is never good.

"Yes. By the 80s the area became densely populated and posed a great health risk. Farms were minimized to make way for housing the population. Indian landowners were threatened with court orders to remove the African families from their land. African landlords were not threatened."

"So, in addition to dismissing the homeland Africans from any say in their country," I said, "they also pitted Black Africans against the Indians, right? And this is around the time the Phoenix Settlement was offering services to the community?"

I understand now why services were so important.

"Yes, people used to bring their grievances to the Settlement. Some were informal hawkers who used to sell on the beach front and were harassed by the police."

"Like the women who sold their scarves and jewelry when we were walking along the promenade last year," I said.

"Yes. Others came with complaints of being victimized by the police for living in the area. Misinformation was being fed to the people telling them that the Indian landowners were threatening to evict them. So, the racial tensions were being fanned constantly by the authorities."

"That means you had poor Indians in the Phoenix township," I said, "and poor tribal Africans in the Inanda region? Correct? And they were right next door to one another?"

"Yes. Sometimes right across the street. There was a stark contrast between two communities of poor people. The Indian poor were brought there from various areas to live in the community-built informal dwellings. They were forced to leave their homes and move to Phoenix Township."

Forced removal. Again, not unlike how native Americans were treated in the U.S.

"They were provided water, electricity, and sanitation but had to pay for these services," she said. "The Inanda residents had no water, electricity, sanitation services, or schools. They could see the development from across the road but could not access the services. This led to growing tensions between the Indian and African communities."

"A setup for a fight over resources," I said.

Isn't that a classic tactic of the schoolyard bully? To pit people against one another.

"In August 1984," she said, "a prominent United Democratic Front leader, Victoria Mxenge (um-eng-gee), was assassinated outside her home. Fear, anxiety, and militancy gripped the people. The forces were now clearly divided between the proponents and opposers of apartheid. Violence broke out throughout the country."

She had been out of 8 ½ years of house arrest for only two years, and now she had to face this?

"We had refugees from both sides at the Settlement. In 1985, we housed a group of Black African refugees in the Printing Press. The local Indian residents offered assistance to them. The Inanda community, now densely populated, made demands for water, sanitation and other services, but the apartheid government rejected these. In 1985 the Zululand homeland authorities took a stand. They said that the area had not been designated for a particular race group, therefore no authority was prepared to provide assistance to the community. In addition, as long as the Indian community refused to move from the area, it would never be designated an African settlement. Their leader said the time had come to forcibly remove the Indians from the area."

Oh, dear. My hand clasped my chest. I was leaning so far over the table I almost knocked over the recorder.

"In August 1985," she said, "Indian homes in the entire Inanda area were targeted and burned down by huge mobs. Eyewitnesses have said that among the people were some who spoke a foreign language. Maybe they were apartheid supporters from neighboring countries, such as Angola or Mozambique."

Loud chanting. Screaming. Angry voices. The acrid smell of burning wood.

"This happened systematically each day from Sunday 4th August. On Friday 9th August, they came to Phoenix Settlement. Some people who had visited Phoenix on Friday and Saturday managed to salvage some of the articles from the museum."

She is talking non-stop, as if transported to a different place and time, as if reliving the experience.

"A second attack on the Settlement," I said. "I remember you said your brother came and picked you up at school during an earlier riot."

"This was much worse," she said. "The Indian families living at the Phoenix Settlement felt they were safe because it was a well-respected Holy site. But the new residents of Inanda and others who came into the country did not know anything about the history of the place nor its significance and its historic relationship with the neighboring communities. They attacked it as if it were any other Indian owned land. They marched on to the property at about mid-day. By then some of the residents of Phoenix had already left. Others fled, and then the place was vandalized and burnt."

"How frightening," I said.

"Sarvodaya, the Gandhi home, was razed to the ground. Only the foundation was left. On Sunday, 11th August, hundreds of people were brought by trucks, shown pieces of land, and told to build their houses on the property. We never learned who brought them and from where. Within a few days the entire 100 acres of Phoenix Settlement land was occupied, including the houses that were still standing and the area around Sarvodaya."

"So, all the green shanty houses, the informal housing I have seen all around the property were not there when you were a child growing up?"

"Correct," she said.

So, the heritage site today is only a small portion of the original settlement.

"What did you do?" I said.

"My sister, Sita, made calls to the police and authorities, but they were unheeded. I visited the Settlement on Thursday before the violence occurred and rescued some of the refugees who we suspected would be targeted and killed. I also told the other residents to leave their homes as we were now helpless in providing protection to them and therefore some left their homes before the devastation."

Thank goodness.

"On Monday 12th, after the attack, I visited the Settlement and was shocked and deeply saddened to see the looting, vandalism, and devastation. I felt helpless because the people there were strangers to me. There was a militancy in them that I was unable to deal with. No one threatened me, but the looting of Gandhi's home, Sarvodaya, continued in my presence."

This is the second time I've wanted to cry during our interviews.

"Doors, door frames, wood from the walls and flooring, and iron from the ceiling were systematically dismantled and carried away brazenly in our presence and in the presence of some foreign journalists who had accompanied me. It was painful to watch. I felt helpless. I felt anger, hurt, and amazement, all the emotions at the same time. But above all, I felt the frustration of being totally helpless against this travesty."

"May I give you a hug?" I stood up.

"You may," she said.

I don't know if this hug is more for her or for me.

Ela took a sip of her now cold tea and resumed her story. "It is a surprise that no one was hurt during the original six days of violence," she said. "Some people left just in time before the violence started. Some prominent Indians drove heavily armored vehicles into the area to rescue families and their belongings prior to the attack. The houses were looted and burned or occupied, so the Indian owners wouldn't return."

How devastating. Everything you have worked you whole life for, now gone.

"There were militant Indian and African groups who confronted each other," she said. "There could have been a bloodbath, but the Indian leaders quickly quelled the militant Indians from attacking. Sadly, many people were killed in the aftermath."

I am so privileged. I have never faced anything close to this level of strife.

"This was a result of internal problems between the divergent groups who began to occupy the land. Drug peddling, illicit landlords or 'shack lords' emerged, and in the months and years that followed the place became crime ridden and violent. The nurses and doctors," she said, "refused to continue work at the clinic on the Settlement because of the threats from the community. Two Indian people who drove to make some deliveries into the Inanda area were killed after an altercation. The rest of the violence was among the African people themselves, and it would appear that this was both criminal as well as political."

"It seems to happen that way," I said. "We saw that in the U.S., when looters began to exploit business owners in their own communities."

"Activists in the Phoenix and Verulam areas organized shelters for the refugees. We were all involved in collection of clothes, equipment for purposes of cooking and sleeping, food, and counseling services for the families. We wrote letters of appeal seeking assistance from various sources and from the government departments. We sought protection for the people while also organizing our own as the government police services were not trusted. However, in the riots that continued around the country many lives were lost, largely African."

How does one segue from a discourse like that? Her pain is still obvious.

A series of knocks at the door shook me out of my reverie. One set of raps louder than the other. The door burst open and in walked two school-age children.

"Hello Ba," said Ela's grandchildren. They hugged her, threw their book bags on the floor or chair, and generally behaved like any child just released from school. She introduced me to her grand-children. A boy and a girl. Both polite and well-spoken. Their chatter turned to more modern things.

"How did you get here?" They each hugged her in turn.

"Our friend's mother dropped us off," said the boy.

"Mummy is late getting into the airport," said the girl.

"She's coming to pick us up just now," said the boy. "Her plane was delayed in landing."

"Why was it delayed?" Ela's voice contained a hit of concern.

"Because the plane was on fire," they said in unison. "But she is fine."

The Gandhi story remains dramatic.

I left Ela to deal with the cheerful energy and the homework that needed supervision while the children waited for their mother, one of Ela's twin daughters, to pick them up.

I took a taxi to DUT for our farewell visit with Strini, Nan, and Lavern. Upon entering Strini's office, I noticed my green suitcase.

"Strini, my suitcase is still here from last year," I said.

"Oh, yes," he said. "I have not had a chance to take it to the school."

"I would be happy to drive you first thing in the morning," said Nan.

"That should work because our plane doesn't leave until later in the day," said Gwen.

I took the suitcase of books and materials for the school to our hotel.

The next morning, Nan picked me up as planned. We drove to the school. It was wonderful to see everyone again. They were thrilled to be receiving books and teaching materials. I laid the suitcase down, grabbed the zipper, pulled it around the edges, and opened it wide.

Are you kidding me? My keys. A year later my wayward keys found me.

Chapter 22

A Mother's Worst Nightmare

From the end of May to August 2011, Ela and I exchanged emails. I was back in Atlanta and would not be visiting Durban again for five months. But I had hours of audiotapes to transcribe, not to mention teaching, conducting research, attending meetings, and writing—always writing.

Early April 2011

RE: Next

 Susan

TO: Ela

Dear Ela,

Once again, you have given me much to think about and a considerable number of hours to transcribe.

I'm working on the transcripts from the second set of interviews. Do you have any questions remaining from the first set? Feel free to make any comments you want.

 Ela Gandhi

TO: Susan

Hello Susan,

What are the little numbers that pop up every few lines?

RE: Next

 Susan

TO: Ela

Dear Ela,

Timing marks from my cassette recorder. Those are the hours, minutes, and seconds into the interview where I would find your comments. That way I can listen again and make sure I am getting things right.

 Ela Gandhi

TO: Susan

Hello Susan,

Here is the first set back. I have corrected spellings of names and dates.

RE: Next

 Susan

TO: Ela

Hi Ela,

Thank you.

Mid-April 2011

RE: Next

 Susan

TO: Ela

Dear Ela,

I have been thinking quite a bit about the violence you experienced. It seems you are fortunate to be alive.

 Ela Gandhi

TO: Susan

Dear Susan,

Once when traveling with a colleague from parliament to our residence at about 5 p.m. my car suddenly stalled and stopped. I was on the right side of the road but close to the pavement. My friend and I sat in the car waiting for the Automobile Association's van to come out to help us. Several cars passed us and offered help, but we told them that we were waiting for AA. Then one young man passed us, parked his car in front of our car and approached us. He pleaded with me to get off the car. At first, I was anxious as to why he was so persistent. Eventually I agreed and got off and asked my friend to come down as well and we waited on the pavement. She had to climb over the gears and come down. No sooner she was standing beside me on the pavement than a huge car came at great speed and banged into my car which in turn smashed into a light pole close by. Had we been in the car we would have been crushed to death. The car was a write off. The young man had left us after asking us to get off. We were stunned and just thanked God for saving us. Was the man an angel? I do not know. My children told me I have seven lives because I have had so many more such experiences.

Later April 2011

RE: Next

 Susan

TO: Ela

Dear Ela,

I have almost finished typing up the latest interview. You said something I'd like to follow up. You spoke about informal housing. And I have heard several others refer to people as informal people? This concept stymies me. How can one person be formal while another exists informally? We are either sentient in this 3-dimensional world or not. Formal recognition, or lack thereof, does not change the fact that we must eat and sleep, or that we are subject to the elements, or to the need for care and attention. Said differently, how can a human being be less than a human being? How can some people live formally, meaning "on the grid" while others are relegated to the status of the animals that run through the forests and fields? It's a sad concept, and I struggle with it.

 Ela Gandhi

TO: Susan

Hello Susan,

The word "informal" refers to the housing and not the people. A brick and tile house with electricity and water would be considered formal. A wood and iron shack with no water or electricity is considered informal.

RE: Next

 Susan

TO: Ela

Hello Ela,

I understand. But what about when one person refers to another as informal? I heard this quite a few times in Durban. You mentioned to me that the Special Forces referred to Indians, Blacks, and Coloureds as snakes. This dehumanized the people so police could brutalize them. I mean, who doesn't want to squash a snake? Especially you. And I have heard several people say things like, "informal people live there." I think it is a hugely important distinction.

 Ela Gandhi

TO: Susan

Hello Susan,

Words have great power to influence the lives of others, and these words, seemingly so simple, are terms that categorize others. People all over the world categorize one another in this manner. For instance, in the US you have Harlem, and there is an image that is created about living in that area. Gandhiji said, "There is nothing more potent than thought. Deed follows word and word follows thought. The world is the result of a mighty thought, and where the thought is mighty and pure, the result is always mighty and pure." And so, yes, referring to a person as informal would be wrong because it dehumanizes them. The thought influences the word, and the word influences the deed.

RE: Next

 Susan

TO: Ela

Hi Ela,

I agree. I have heard it said that if you don't like the outcome, change your mind. I think that was a tenet of the Theosophical Society. It makes sense he would embrace that. So, if you think of people as less than human, like they did in Rwanda, they called people cockroaches, then the thought produced a word, and the word allowed the atrocious deed of genocide. Words matter.

I can't help thinking about my adopted son. He's Rwandan. Raised in a Ugandan refugee camp, came to the U.S. for an education, earned his master's degree. He's back in Rwanda now, has an excellent job in the technology industry, a wife, and three precious children. They are the children of my heart. The perpetrators of the Rwandan genocide referred to their victims as cockroaches. Now the country has strict rules against asking about another's heritage, whether Hutu or Tutsi, because it doesn't matter. One's race does not matter. Thinking it matters causes hurtful words, and hurtful words result in heinous deeds. Thoughts generate words, and words yield deeds.

May 2011

RE: Next

 Susan

TO: Ela

Hello again.

I have the written transcripts of the last interview. I need to tweak them a bit, then I will send them to you. I went through them and saw some holes where I didn't explore things well enough. Would you mind if I asked a few more questions?

 Ela Gandhi

TO: Susan

Dear Susan,

I would be happy to answer as best as I can.

RE: Next

 Susan

TO: Ela

Hi,

We talked about your life in the 70s and into the 80s up to the burning of the Phoenix Settlement. But we haven't talked about the period of time between the burning and the end of apartheid. I suspect things were really rough.

I'm sure there were continued clashes between whites and non-whites, Indians and homeland Africans, and as you said, among the tribal territories. Would you tell me what happened from the destruction of the settlement to Mandela's release? So, end of the 80s to mid-90s.

 Ela Gandhi

TO: Susan

Hello Susan,

You are right. It was not an easy time. In fact, it was the worst time.

I mentioned that two of my children chose to live in Verulam with their father. On 16th December 1993, Kush, my second son was assassinated in that house. We were preparing to go to elections and lots of violence and political tensions were occurring in KwaZulu Natal. Kush was alone at home when some people came to the house, stole his car and TV, and shot him. He was found dead in what the police called a robbery but there were many indicators to point out that this was not a robbery. If they wanted a TV, there was one downstairs. They didn't need to go upstairs for a TV. They could have taken the TV and car and other things and gone. But they went upstairs for that TV, and they shot him. What was the need?

After the end of apartheid, the new government established The Truth and Reconciliation Commission (TRC) in 1995. Their purpose was to investigate victims and perpetrators. Their first report was released in 1998 and their final report 2003. They established a moratorium period in which people could confess their crimes and have them removed from the record with no penalty. They wrote to us a letter and said this was a political assassination and the file was closed. There was no indication as to who was responsible or what was the reason. It is a sad part of our lives.

This just does me in. My own son is in his 20s, like her son was. If this had happened to him, I would be traumatized for the remainder of my life. I'm crying for her, for my fear, and for the all the mothers who lost children in this struggle, and all the mothers today who are losing children to violence based on their race.

RE: Next

 Susan

TO: Ela

Hi Ela,

I am so saddened to learn this. When we came to your house for dinner on my first trip to Durban, you showed me your late son's picture. I didn't realize this occurred in such a shocking way. Did you ask the TRC to reconsider the decision? Wouldn't you like to see the perpetrators in prison or punished or worse?

 Ela Gandhi

TO: Susan

Yes, we asked, but they said it was behind us now. No, I would not seek revenge if the perpetrators were found by asking for their lives to be taken. After receiving the TRC statement that my son's killing was politically motivated, I have received no further word. No further action took place. No one was ever charged in the assassination. No one ever stepped forward to accept responsibility. No one stepped forward during the moratorium. No clear reason was ever identified for this crime. But the truth is out there.

Many issues were addressed this way. The information was repressed in an effort to move the peace process forward. And that was that. What good would retribution or violence do? My grandfather said that victory attained by violence is tantamount to a defeat, for it is momentary.

The people who did this may have been the victors in that moment, but they have to live with themselves and their actions the rest of their lives.

RE: Next

 Susan

TO: Ela

I admire your ability to accept things as they are. There is a popular saying in the U.S. right now: "It is what it is." Lots of people say it, but the grace and peace you have summoned from deep within takes this to another whole level. I will have to think about this for a while. Thank you for showing me what it means to be merciful and kind.

Ela has such a deep understanding of what Mohandas Gandhi meant when he said, "Truth is God." She has a fundamental acceptance that the truth of this needless murder is known at some Universal level. It is the only sense I can make of the unresolved trauma this family endures. The powers that be shrugged their shoulders, cavalierly attributing it to the zeitgeist of the times. They washed their hands of further action. But Ela modeled a living example of a most courageous act of the acceptance of Truth, with a capital T. Universal Truth, not little t, ego-based truth.

June 2011

RE: Next

 Susan

TO: Ela

Ela,

Here are the transcripts for the March 2011 interviews. Please feel free to make changes, as you did with the first set. I am sure I spelled many of the names wrong.

I have another question. I looked on the web at what was happening at the end of apartheid. In the most recent interview, you said a vote was attempted in 1984. This was not successful because all the race groups were not included. So, the apartheid government went out, finally, and the new bicameral government came in. The two chambers are the National Assembly (NA) and the National Council of Provinces (NCP). And you were on the parliament from 1994 to 2004. So that means you represented KZN on the NCP. More alphabet soup.

My question is this: Other than agreeing to a two-chamber government, were there problems with the voting? There was still a lot of animosity and aggression going on, I am sure.

Oh my gosh, I just realized. Her son was murdered in 1993, and she became a parliamentarian in 1994. That required an amazing strength of conviction and ability to set one's own pain aside to work for relief in the rest of the country. So much in a short period of time. Unsuccessful election 1984, Phoenix burned 1985, divorce 1987, visits Mandela in prison, 1990, son's murder 1993, on the parliament of the new government 1994. Such commitment. So very Gandhi.

 Ela Gandhi

TO: Susan

Susan,

You are right. There was still a lot of violence, and we still needed to make sure there was no election tampering. A Transitional Executive Council (TEC) was created in 1993, and I was a member. We had a 60-person Commonwealth Observer Group (COG) who monitored the voting, security of persons and ballots, and ensured the legality of the process. The government was instituted, and Nelson Mandela was chosen as its first president. It was a wonderful relief to most people. Mandela was president from 1994 to 1999. Through all of this, there was still turmoil and violence.

RE: Next

 Susan

TO: Ela

Amazing. Yes, I remember. You told the audience when you were in Atlanta that you set a record in the first five years for changing laws. And you did all of this while traveling back and forth between Cape Town and Durban. I'm exhausted just thinking of it.

At lunch one day with Sue and Gwen, I was discussing this email.

"I have a question for you," I said. "Who was the last apartheid leader before the 1994 election?"

"That would be de Klerk," Gwen said. "He was president of the National Party from 1989 to 1994. He was a conservative, but toward the end, his perspective changed, and he agreed apartheid should end."

"Ela said there was still turmoil and violence as the new government settled in," I said.

"Yes," said Sue. "Did you know that de Klerk's first wife was stabbed and strangled to death in 2001 in her flat in Cape Town?" "No!" I said. "That's terrible."

"Yes," she said. "The source I read said it was a disgruntled 21-year-old. He was an indigenous African and a security guard at the community where she was living."

Probably a member of that group of disenfranchised souls referred to as "informal."

Chapter 23

Zulu Boys and Ashes

In August of 2011, we returned to Durban.

Entering the Elangeni Hotel felt like a homecoming. The lobby was bustling with guests coming and going. A social event was taking place in the hotel ballroom. Perhaps a wedding, as some of the guests were dressed in formal attire.

The young ladies wore dresses of taffeta or organza and lace. Many wore brightly colored fascinators in their hair, complete with feathers or flowers matching the vivid colors of their dresses. The young men looked proud in their formal tuxedos, backs straight, heads up. Or maybe they were just compensating for the tightness of their bow ties.

Sue, Gwen, and now Dr. Julie Washington from GSU, and I met Ela and Lavern for dinner in the hotel's restaurant. Julie is a renowned expert on reading disabilities from a community perspective in elementary school aged African American children. She was a perfect addition to the existing team. This was to be my final trip. Hayward and Janice remained in Atlanta.

"Look," said Sue. "It's our old table, and nobody is there. Let's take it for old-time's sake." She dashed off to lay claim to the table where we had dined many times before.

"Hello," said Lavern. His strong and mellow voice called to us from across the restaurant. He and Ela had arrived. Gwen crossed the room to greet them. They returned and we all sat down, chatting away like children who hadn't seen their friends in a while.

"Tell me of your agenda this week," said Ela. She was sitting at her usual place at the end of the table. She wore a new Punjabi outfit, green-hued this time.

"Our plan," said Gwen, "is to visit some old schools, do workshops for some new schools, and take a trip up to the region y'all call, "The Bush." The waiter came by and filled our water glasses.

"And I plan to meet with community administrators," I said, "to ask for letters of support for a U.S. Agency for International Development (USAID) grant proposal I hope to write when I get back to Atlanta." I looked at the menu, searching for any new dishes. I had never been disappointed in this restaurant.

"We're hoping it will assist the Ixopo region in improving literacy," said Sue.

"What is the goal of your grant proposal?" Lavern's question contained sincere interest.

Same old Lavern. That regal posture never changes.

"The goal," I said, "would be to develop a series of books for early childhood classrooms. The process involves encouraging interactions between children and their parents and grandparents, leveraging a language technique called 'elaborative reminiscing.'"

"We would ask older members of the community," said Julie, "to relay stories from their childhood and translate these into English. This technique has the potential to improve children's literacy in the context of their cultural heritage." She was wearing a beautiful, chunky turquoise necklace. She has the face and air to carry off big jewelry.

"Julie is our expert on literacy and culture," I said. "We are so lucky she could join us."

After dinner, I moved to a seat closer to Ela to talk with her. "It's so wonderful to see you again, Ela," I said. "I'm sure you know what I'm going to say."

"You have more questions for me," she said. She raised an eyebrow and smiled.

"Always more questions," I said.

I'm tired of me, so I am sure she is as well.

"We will try to find a time to meet while you are here," she said. "Perhaps a lunch one day."

"Thank you," I said.

Someone dropped a tray of dishes. All eyes turned to the source of the noise, then quickly back to conversations. We were enjoying reconnecting. The evening ended with another round of hugs and we all went our separate ways. Ela and Lavern to their homes, Gwen, Sue, Julie, and I to our rooms.

The next day we drove to our first school in two cars. Ela was not with us. She would drive her own vehicle later. Our first stop was the Hlutankunga (hloo-tan-kuhn-ga) School. As we walked up the hill toward the school, a group of young boys was playing a war game.

"I'm Shaka," shouted one boy. He raised a fisted stick in the air. "And you are my subjects now." He herded small groups of children into a larger group, an imaginary spear thrusting at them to poke them along. He continued simulating the actions of King Shaka, who united the tribes in KwaZulu Natal under one leader.

"See here," shouted another boy. "Now it is my turn to be Shaka."

So cute. Similar to the way children in the U.S. pretend to be Power Rangers or Marvel heroes.

We proceeded to the administration building, once again greeted by the warm smiles of our friend, Mrs. Norris. This time Julie had the pleasure of meeting the children, hearing their songs and orations, and getting a feel for the needs of the school.

"These children need books," she said. Wide-eyed recognition of the challenges these teachers faced dawned in her awareness, as it had in our previous visit.

"I have a contact at a major children's publishing house," she said. "I am sure I can get them to send several boxes."

We drove onward toward our next school. A high school this time. On the way we passed through an enclave of cement houses, interspersed with rondavels. Each main rondavel had one to five

Local Scene

connected outer structures. They looked like little clusters of mushrooms, one outer building for each wife, we were told. In addition to the cement houses and clusters of rondavels, there was an iron and wooden structure, which appeared to be a common building.

We got out of the car to look out at the rolling hills. Off in the distance we heard young men's voices chanting in unison. We peered toward the dirt path running down a hill behind a tall tree. The chanting grew louder, the group of men closer. We saw the tops of spears as the group came up the path, then the tops of heads as they marched up the incline behind the tree.

"Maybe we should get back in the car," I said. I was unnerved by the spears waving in the air.

"I don't know," said Gwen. "Maybe move closer to it, just in case."

We backed away from the side of the dirt road, edging closer to the car. Now their heads were fully in sight. About a dozen or more young men, chanting, waving their spears in our direction. None of us spoke. We just stared, wide-eyed.

If they are wearing skins and furs like the dancers at UShaka beach, I'm going to freak out.

The leader of the group drew closer to the top of the rise. We could see their shirts now. All different colors. I wasn't expecting that.

As they ascended to the top of the rise, we saw each wearing a tee shirt. Common logos for popular soft drinks, various sports teams, sneaker companies, and technology titans adorned their shirts. As they reached the summit of the path, it was clear there were no skins, furs, or feathers. Only blue jeans.

T-shirts and blue jeans. Standard young person's attire all over the world.

But they still kept coming toward us, chanting and brandishing spears. *This can't be real. This cannot be the way my life ends. I'll never be a grandmother.* The young men marched through the tall grass, toward us, and then they marched right on past the car. No stopping. No asking who we were. No aggression.

"That was intense," said Sue. The group marched on down the road. "Not in a million years did I expect that."

Are you embarrassed now? You should be.

We got in the car and drove onward, past the little village, and up the hillside to the school, where we would conduct our workshops and give our presentations once more. Entering the parking lot, we noticed a car emblazoned with the word, "Satyagraha." Ela arrived before we did.

"Ela," I said. "You won't believe what just happened. A small army of young men came at us, waving spears."

"Oh," she said. She waved the back of her hand and me, dismissing the thought. "That's nothing to fret about. They are having their annual competition commemorating King Shaka's victory."

Whew. Just a bigger boy version of the games the littler boys were playing on the school ground.

We entered the building, met the teachers and staff, conducted our presentations, and left.

As I walked past Ela's car, I noticed a picture of her in a newspaper on the front dashboard. She was on a boat and all dressed in white.

"I didn't mean to be snoopy," I said, "But I noticed this picture of you on a boat." I pointed toward the paper. Her eyes followed.

"Do you like boating," I said. "Maybe next time you come to Atlanta I can take you for a ride on our lake."

"No," she said. "Goodness, no." Her hand shot up and clutched her throat. "I can't swim. That was taken when we dispersed Gandhiji's ashes into the ocean last year." Her hand relaxed its grip.

Gwen waved at me. Our car was ready to leave. "Gotta go," I said. I jogged toward the car, twisting slightly to wave back at her. "Maybe you can tell me about it when we meet next."

"You can read about it in the newspapers," she said. Her voice was slightly raised to cover the distance.

Back at the hotel, I pulled out my laptop and typed in "Gandhi's Ashes Durban." I opened a Reuters website.

Several websites recounted the same event. At the time of Gandhi's death, his ashes were disseminated among friends and family members and were even carried on a country-wide tour to help heal the grieving nation. One person removed some of the ashes as a memento. Upon this person's death, the little urn of ashes passed into Ela's hands.

On that anniversary day, members of the Navy carried several boatloads of family members and friends out into the harbor, where Ela dispersed the ashes to their final resting place.

This was to be my last interaction with Ela in South Africa. For whatever reason, we did not have the opportunity to meet again. On the plane ride home, I developed another list of questions to send her via email.

RE: another question

 Susan

TO: Ela

Dear Ela,

I read about the dispersal of your grandfather's ashes. I see that standing up to the Navy generals led to a good outcome. You have a special relationship with the Navy, which came in handy.

You told me you don't swim. Were you afraid?"

 Ela Gandhi

TO: Susan

Hello Susan,

This was on the 68th anniversary of his death. My daughter, Ashish, was very concerned that I may fall overboard. But I guessed with all those healthy young Navy men and women around, if I fell, someone would save me.

Chapter 24

Ela's Letter on Satyagraha

It was the end of September 2011.

I love to travel, but it's great to be back home.

"Back at the computer already, I see," said Dewey. He was seated at the window.

"Not for long," I said. I pointed out the window. "Look at how the sun glistens off the lake, like little crystal shards. My poor flowers didn't fare well while we were gone. They dried up in the intense Georgia heat." We watched a fishing boat pass by.

"The yellow jackets are out in full force," he said. He moved away from the window just as a bee decided to dive-bomb it.

"Yes," I said, "but their season ends soon, and the old queen will die. The trees and bushes are so dense here, unlike Kwa Zulu Natal."

"You know I'm in love with Ela," Dewey said. "Have you heard anything from her lately?" He gave me a wink.

"That's OK," I said, "So am I. I'm not worried." I winked back. "I'm just finishing up my list of follow-up questions for her from my last trip."

"Well, tell her I said 'hi' when you email her," he said. He left the room. The buzzing of the bees outside was loud enough to hear through the window.

"Will do," I said. My attention returned to the computer.

RE: another question

 Susan

TO: Ela

Hi Ela,

It was wonderful to see you again.

Sue and Gwen just confirmed that you will be here in April to give a speech at the Blurring Boundaries conference. I can't wait to see you again. ☺

I have another question.

You have spoken briefly about the idea of Satyagraha. This is the theme for your current movement. I remember seeing it on your car.

Would you please tell me about the idea, how it started, and how you envision it today?

Dewey says hi.

 Ela Gandhi

TO: Susan

Hello Susan,

I wrote this as a document and attached it because the answer is long.

I picked up my laptop and went to my father's assisted living home for the day. In addition to the regular staff, he hired a "secretary" to take care of his "paperwork." She was ill, so I went instead. He was physically frail and losing ground in the memory department.

"Hey Daddy," I said. "Ela wrote me a letter about Satyagraha. Would you like me to read it to you?" I held up my laptop so he could see the letter was not on paper.

"Humpf," he said. "That's not a letter." He turned away, looking out the window at his bird feeder.

"It's a modern-day letter, Daddy," I said. I tilted my head and raised my eyebrows.

"Sure," he said. "Why not." I fluffed his pillow so he could sit up.

"OK," I said. "Here goes."

Ela's Letter

> The Satyagraha movement started on September 11, 1906 in Johannesburg. Gandhiji was 37 at that time. The government then was not the same as we have now. The Provinces of Natal and Cape were ruled by English-speaking British people. The Republic of the Orange Free State and the South African Republic, or the Transvaal as they called it then, were ruled over by the Afrikaner Dutch people.

"The Dutch people are very nice," Dad said. "I had some business over there once. Great time." He turned toward me. I had jogged a memory.

> In 1910 the Union of South Africa was declared, where all provinces came together. At that time, Africans could not move from Natal to the Transvaal without a pass, called a dompass.
>
> A bill was put forth to prohibit Indians from crossing the border as well. There was one government, but it applied controls differently to different people. You had to give your 5-finger imprints like a criminal, you know. And you had to produce a whole lot of documents, as if you were charged of a crime. Gandhiji established protests against this. It went to court in Johannesburg because people did not want to submit to passes.

"You had to go to court?" Dad said. "When?"

"No, Daddy," I said. "Gandhi went to court." I shook my head and looked back at the screen.

> People's emotions were so aroused that they stood up and took an oath in a mass meeting. They said, "In the name

of God we will not submit to this law." Prior to this, Gandhiji talked about passive resistance, but after this oath he was quite moved and said "now we brought God into this. It's not just us, it's also God involved in the whole situation. As a result, he felt that now this movement couldn't be called passive resistance.

It was a very active, well thought-out resistance and so he said the people needed to have another name for it.

He advertised in the newspaper for a name and invited people to write an essay about the movement and to suggest a name.

"I had a newspaper once," Dad said. "Remember when you were kids and rolled them up for me?" Another memory.

"Sure do," I said. "I forgot to tell Ela about that. Let's move on, Daddy." I read slowly, almost melodiously to keep his attention.

They came up with the name, Sadagraha. This means 'force of truth,' but then Gandhiji changed it to Satyagraha, which was easier to pronounce and means 'insistence on truth.' In 1913, there was a huge march in South Africa, held to insist on the truth that all people should have similar rights, not just the whites, whether British or Afrikaner. Thousands of people crossed over the border into the Transvaal in protest of many grievances. For example, the government imposed a three £ (pound) tax on the freed indentured workers, which was difficult for them to afford. Indenture became a revolving door. They could not afford the fee, so signed for additional indenture.

"Did you know your 7th great grandfather came over on the Mayflower?" Dad said.

Where's that coming from?

"Yes," I said. I recognized the connection he made. "He was an indentured servant, right?"

"Yes," he said. "Don't tell your mother." I had to stifle a huge laugh.

They also forbade and would not recognize traditional Hindu or Muslim marriages. Their wives were not considered to be their spouses, and their children were considered illegitimate and therefore had no rights. So, the protest march of 1913, conducted primarily by women, culminated in all three points being resolved: the government withdrew the three £ tax, they recognized marriages from other religious traditions, and they stopped the dompasses. That was the beginning of Satyagraha.

Dad said nothing. He was staring at the blank TV.

In 1996, I decided I would like to run a newspaper, which would be largely aimed at transforming the Indian community.

"Good for her," Dad said. "You tell her I'm proud of her." I stopped to help him move from the bed to the chair. Then we continued.

With this idea in mind, we started a newspaper called 'Satyagraha in Pursuit of Truth.' The paper looks at basic issues that concerned communities would not read in normal papers. It goes to both the Indian and African communities but has a much wider readership than this. The first edition came out in 2000. The mainline media was not giving the correct story.

"They never do," Dad said. He shook his fist in the air.

We couldn't just sit on the fence and say things are wrong and not have an alternative to tell the people. What was the alternative? You have a new government, but that new government has limited resources and can't attend to everybody's need in one go.
For example, in South Africa before the new government, people were living shunted to rural areas. Once the new government came in, people flooded the urban areas and there was no housing for them.

"Well, you don't need to buy it for them," Dad said.

Sometimes he's so connected and other times he's in his own little world.

There were no schools for African people. There were beautiful schools for White people, fairly good schools for Indians and Coloureds, but with African people, there were no schools. They had no health facilities, either. There was a conflict of maintenance of the old facilities while establishing the new. Money was the main problem.

"It always is," Dad said.

Further, the unemployment rate amongst African people was around 80% on average if you counted the rural and urban areas–80%! For Indians and Coloured people the unemployment rate was about 15% and for White people there was no unemployment.

"Well that's just a shame, isn't it," Dad said. "A man's gotta work." He shook his head and clucked his tongue.

Before the end of apartheid, every white person who wanted a job had some employment because of the concept of sheltered employment.

Certain jobs went only to white people. You didn't train Indians, Coloured people and African people to be engineers. They were boiler makers or plumber's assistants. Indians were carpenters.

"Your great grandfather was a carpenter," Dad said." He was fussing with the edge of his old sweater, picking off the fuzz balls.

"I didn't know that," I said.

And so, after apartheid, Black Africans were getting trained, which meant they were taking jobs the Indians and Coloureds used to do, and the Indians and Coloureds started to feel sidelined and marginalized.

This led to misunderstandings and violence because they didn't understand the history of the situation. So, we felt a newspaper could give education and raise awareness in the community. That was the idea behind the Satyagraha newspaper. We began with no staff. We used to do all the work and we spent our own money as well. We collected from amongst ourselves.

"Same with my little paper," Dad said. He folded and refolded some papers.

I did all the stories and together with another friend we did all the layout for the newspaper. We would take it to the printers, and so the cost was only printing. Layout, stories, all of that was voluntary work. Then in 2002, we received some money from the Mott Foundation. This allowed us to employ a journalist, to grow from a 4-pager to an 8-pager, and to begin our own distribution network. We now have a circulation of 20,000 and are hoping to increase it to 30-35,000. We don't have a copyright because we feel knowledge should be shared.

The floor nurse came into the room just as I finished the letter. "This is my daughter, Susan," Dad said, for the umpteenth time. "She would like to buy the world a Coke."

He may have missed the details, but he got the message of service.

Later, at home, I emailed Ela about the paper.

RE: another question

(**S**) Susan

TO: Ela

What kinds of topics do you cover in the newspaper?

(**EG**) Ela Gandhi

TO: Susan

Satyagraha covers a range of topics from remembrance pieces of great leaders such as Chief Albert Luthuli and King, to the listeriosis and malaria outbreaks, to preparations for the Salt March, to problems with the national power grid, and even to a recipe for corn fritters from my kitchen.

RE: another question

 Susan

TO: Ela

Hi Ela,

How do people get copies of the paper?

 Ela Gandhi

TO: Susan

The entire collection is on the Gandhi Development Trust website under 'electronic media.' You can find it by going to http://www.satyagraha.org.za. If you register on the website, you can read all the issues.

Chapter 25

The Aftermath

The day after I read Ela's letter about Satyagraha to Dad, I sent another question.

RE: another question

 Susan

TO: Ela

Dear Ela,

Thank you for your answer about Satyagraha. Dewey says hi.

Your discussion of Satyagraha brings up another question. Would you please describe the history and purpose of the Gandhi Development Trust?

EG Ela Gandhi

TO: Susan

Hello,

The primary objective of the GDT is to keep Gandhi's principles alive. To promote them locally and in the world.

Yes

We work closely with Satyagraha to reach out to schools, where we conduct a speech and essay competition in 7th and 10th grades. Our topics are usually current issues but with a Gandhian point of view. For example, this year we asked participants to talk about what Gandhi would have done about climate change.

What a great idea.

We conduct these competitions in two languages: English and Zulu.

We also conduct a Salt March Commemoration. The Salt March was an act of civil disobedience Gandhi led in 1930 against the salt tax in India. The commemoration began in 2005 on the 75th anniversary of Gandhiji's march. It also was the year of the 50th anniversary of the South African Freedom Charter. We felt this was an important focus for the marches because peace is not just a selfish look at your own needs but also the needs of others.

Such an important concept.

In our first few marches we had the South African Defense Force marching with us. After the 22-kilometer march and our speeches, the colonel literally cried. The message at the end promotes non-violence and Ubuntu. He was so overcome with the experience, and with the idea of peace and non-violence.

A difficult concept for anyone, but especially for a career colonel.

This was profound because the Defense Force was supposed to be hard nuts. 'Men don't cry.' We felt this was a success. To change a person, to get a person to think about their own roles.

Our message is: How do we create a culture of non-violence? The message at the end of the march promotes both non-violence and Ubuntu, getting people to think about what they can do to change the world, not wait for other people to do something.

I love this.

The Gandhi Development Trust also organizes annual lectures on the 30th of January, the day Gandhiji was assassinated. We work to find more and better dialogue with other religions, other race groups, to meet the challenges of, for example, climate change and how we can conserve the environment. We also support a youth day of non-violence on the 2nd of October.

These are a few of the activities.

The Gandhi Development Trust espouses five core values and five working principles. You can read about these on http://www.gdt.org.za/word/gdt-core-values-principles.

Core Values

- Responsibility
- Honesty
- Integrity
- Justice
- Compassion

Principles

- Do as much as you can with less
- Teamwork
- Build partnerships
- Commitment
- Monitor, evaluate and plan

October 2011

RE: another question

 Susan

TO: Ela

Hello,

I love the idea of starting really young because the younger generation is going to inherit all the problems our generation couldn't fix or caused. I know your topic in

April is going to be on the concept of a peace curriculum. I can't wait to hear it.

 Ela Gandhi

TO: Susan

Hello,

Thank you. You are right. There is tremendous pressure on young people. I think young people face a huge challenge because of the way the world is moving. We are all concerned about the fragile nature of the planet. We don't know what is going to happen in the next century—whether we are going to have sufficient resources, whether we are going to have drinking water for the people. There are those people that say the next war will be about access to drinking water. To prevent future disaster, young people need to look at constructive ways of dealing with this rather than becoming violent.

November 2011

RE: another question

(S) Susan

TO: Ela

Hello Ela,

Dewey says hi.

I'm working down the list of questions I generated for your autobiography when I was on the plane last visit. Here's the next.

Some time ago, we talked about the burning of the Phoenix Settlement. The violence and destruction of that event has weighed on my mind. I was wondering how you handled your anger about the situation. How long did it take for you to resolve those feelings?

 Ela Gandhi

TO: Susan

Hello Susan,

Give my regards to Dewey.

I have no anger about what happened. Growing up at Phoenix taught me three very useful lessons.

She's a better person than I am. I would struggle with the anger.

One, the strategies repressive governments used were often not easily understood or comprehended. So, to feel anger against the looters at the Settlement would be misplaced anger.

In what sense?

One had to understand how the oppressive system orchestrated such a terrible pogrom. Was it not to create a wedge between the Indian and African communities, to orchestrate further internecine violence, and to weaken the unity brought about by the United Democratic Front?

OK

Was it not to instill fear and uncertainty?

Was it not to deter Indian people from participating in protest actions against the white government?

Was it not to get the support of the Indian community for the white government, to position themselves as their saviors?

Being angry would not be constructive towards solving the problem and therefore it was important to control the anger.

Very difficult task, indeed.

We needed to analyze the situation and plan how to deal with it, which we did. We coordinated one of the biggest nonracial marches against the apartheid government in 1989. And the unity of the mass democratic movement was consolidated.

Second, I learned from my parents and Gandhiji that it is important to understand people's vulnerabilities and to be able to appropriately reach out to them as a friend and not a foe. Befriend the people, not distance yourself from them.

Even the ones that are so evil? Amazing.

Never lose faith in the people.

Third, I learned that at a time like this, one needed to be calm and compassionate and not brash and impulsive in the way the situation should be handled.

RE: another question

 Susan

TO: Ela

Hello,

Those are such important lessons. They would really help everyone in every situation from family squabbles, to departmental discord, to clashes within communities. Thank you.

Here is my next question.

You mentioned that interlopers and squatters took over the Settlement. How did you reclaim it after it was occupied?

 Ela Gandhi

TO: Susan

Hello Susan,

The three lessons I sent you were very important in that process.

They were shared by some of my friends. One was Richard Steel, who was living on the Settlement at the time. He was a conscientious objector and refused to join the SA army as a conscript. He served imprisonment for his beliefs and is a true Gandhian.

He and his wife helped with the negotiations in the community.

At least she had close friends doing this with her.

Eventually it was agreed that 80 % of the land would be given to the City Council to build properly serviced houses for the people. In turn, the people would move out of the other 20% to make way for the development of a heritage site on the property.

Hardly seems fair to give up so much.

The buildings would be restored, and other facilities would be put up for the use of the community. We needed to raise their consciousness. They needed to understand the importance and significance of the Settlement. But this did not happen because there was much in-fighting during this period.

The community was transient. People would come and then leave because the violence and threats continued.

How do you make any inroads with a group when the members are always changing?

It was only 15 years later in 2000 that an accord with the people was finalized and Phoenix was restored. But much of the 20 acres restored to Phoenix was reoccupied and remains so to this day.

Only 15 years?

At present, there is the Press building which houses a tourism office, an internet café, a computer center, and an education center for young students to engage in reading. Students are offered tuition in specific subjects, on request. Gandhiji's home, Sarvodaya, is restored.

The museum houses an exhibition on Gandhiji's transformation during his 21 years in South Africa. It explains how his ideas evolved in respect to people, to class and caste, to gender, to health, and to what it means to organize popular nonviolent struggles.

Oh, yes. I remember this from our tour.

The museum also depicts the inspiration he derived from philosophers such as Tolstoy and Ruskin and from scriptures of the Bible, the Koran, and the Gita. He also studied books on holistic health and natural remedies such as Henry Salt and others.

Salt. He was big on vegetarianism.

The display also depicts some of the movements around the world that were influenced by Gandhiji's ideas, such as Martin Luther King, the life of Kasturba, Mandela, and many others. My father also built a cement block house when I was young, Kasturba Bhavan. This too was burned and looted. Today it is a place for the elderly in the area to congregate.

An amazing resource to the community. I hope they know that.

Plans for a new building are in the pipeline as are future projects. Once that is accomplished, Kasturba Bhavan will be reconfigured to serve another purpose.

There is also the Kasturba Gandhi Primary School. It has an enrollment of over a thousand children. There is a crèche with about 250 children and a drop-in center at the clinic, offering services to the chronically ill, the indigent, and the vulnerable.

Wow

There are plans to upgrade the present densely populated un-serviced, informal housing. It still creates a health hazard. The Gandhi Development Trust has agreed to donate a further few acres of land for this purpose. But the Council is still busy with the formalities to complete this project. These activities are all in line with the aims and objectives of the Trust, which was drawn up by Mahatma Gandhi in 1913 before he left SA.

Chapter 26

How to Protest

Ela Protesting Graduation Restrictions

The hustle and bustle of the Christmas season was upon us. Nevertheless, Ela continued to answer all my questions.

December 2011

RE: another question

 Susan

TO: Ela

Hi Ela,

Merry Christmas.

I have been reading through all the transcripts and all our emails, and I am trying to come up with a summary of how to protest. You said the difference between Gandhi's movement and others is that he emphasized the need to do constructive work for people, to uplift them, to empower them, to make them self-sufficient. Here is the summary list I have so far. I've put them into an attachment.

(EG) Ela Gandhi

TO: Susan

1. Protests should involve us, not me. Non-violent protests require lots of popular support.

Us, not me

2. Non-violent protest requires extensive planning and groundwork. Go door-to-door and talk with people if needed. Listen to what they say and list the issues before giving feedback and motivating them to take joint action.

Plan and Prepare

a) People need time to state what they want.

b) People need to believe in the cause.

c) They need to be clear about the outcome they are protesting for, so they don't back down at the first sign of resistance from the opponent.

d) It takes a long time to mobilize people.

Take your time

e) People have to believe in their own power. If you doubt the cause, you cannot convince others.

f) Rent-a-crowd protests will never work because of the above.

3. Control your anger. Meet hostility with grace and calmness. Better to make a friend than a foe.

No hostility

4. Deescalate tensions while they are small, otherwise they may intensify. It is easier to stop them before they spiral out of control than to get control after the fact.

Deescalate tension

5. Expect that there will be interlopers who see this as an opportunity for their own profit. Whether to promote a different cause subversively or for pay from an outside force, opportunists will appear. People need to be careful without being confrontational as then splits can occur. We need to try to transform such people and keep them focused and working all the time. It is easy to deal with them if your process is transparent and participatory.

Root out opportunists

6. Non-violent protest is about transforming people on both sides. It takes longer, but it is much better than murder and destruction. Violence leads to more violence.

7. Consider how to address the needs of the other side as well.

Consider needs of both sides

8. Protests should involve constructive action. Don't just present your problems. Work on the solution. Take constructive action to demonstrate what a positive outcome might look like.

January 2012

RE: another question

 Susan

TO: Ela

Hi Ela,

Happy New Year.

Thank you for sprucing up the list. We're going to use this somewhere in your book.

Change of topic.

You told me about house arrest and all your tormenters. I will never forget what you said. You said, "The cause was bigger than all the anger and all the frustration." That has stuck with me. No comment needed. Just sharing.

RE: another question

 Susan

TO: Ela

Hello Again,

I have one last question from our notes and conversations, and then I promise I'll leave you in peace for a while. Have you ever met any of those people who tormented you during apartheid?

 Ela Gandhi

TO: Susan

Hello Susan,

Once after the end of apartheid, I met a policeman who introduced himself as the son of one of the police who had been my tormentors. I asked if his father had been 'the notorious one' and he said yes. The son was not at all remorseful about his father's inhumane treatment of me and of others.

Like father, like son.

> My encounter with him wasn't a very good one. I didn't feel that I could relate to him in any way because he wasn't repentant for what his father had done. He even told me, "Well, you see how the crime is now. In those days of apartheid there was no crime in the country," and I said, "It depends on how you define crime."

To him, a crime was only a crime if it was an action against him. That speaks volumes about human nature. And it is why we will always need non-violent, principled strategies for protest.

Chapter 27

Peace Education

Apr il 2011 came fast. The announcement for the conference had been out for a while.

The Georgia State University College of Education

is hosting Blurring Boundaries: An International Educational Development Conference, on April 10-11, 2012. The conference will be held at the Westin Peachtree Plaza Hotel.

Opening speakers include COE Dean Randy Kamphaus and Ramu Damodaran, deputy director for partnerships and public engagement in the United Nations Department of Public Information

Ela Gandhi, past chancellor of the Durban University of Technology and former member of the South African Parliament, will be speaking on peace education at the plenary session.

The Westin is a gargantuan hotel and conference complex in downtown Atlanta. That's the bad news. The good news is that it is a few short blocks from my office. On the day of Ela's presentation, long tables were set out in lecture fashion in the ballroom, lines of folding chairs snugly shoved underneath.

"Good," I said. We can take notes this way. Sue sat to my left, Gwen to my right.

The conference commenced. The two opening speakers gave their messages. The host introduced Ela.

"Ladies and gentlemen," said the host. "It is my distinct honor to introduce to you our next speaker. A newspaperwoman, member of the South African Parliament, social worker, social justice activist, member of the U.N. Millennial Goals Committee, and grand-daughter of that icon of peace, Mohandas Karamchand Gandhi, she is a peace activist in her own right. Ela Gandhi suffered through the atrocities perpetrated by the South African apartheid government, engaged in actions to bring about the end of apartheid, and participated in crafting the laws and policies of the post-apartheid government. Today she works tirelessly for the establishment of a peace curriculum in schools around the world. Please join me in welcoming Ela Gandhi."

There was polite applause.

"Scoot your chair over a little," Sue said. "You can't see through that guy in front of you."

"She looks so tiny next to the announcer," said Gwen. "He's over 6' tall, and she's just 5'2. He towers over her."

The crowd noticed this as Ela walked up to the podium. It sent a soft chuckle through the room.

"Hello Everybody," said Ela. She began this speech the way she began the interview with Donna Lowry. Her voice was soft, high-pitched, somewhat wavery.

"Hello," said the audience. They mimicked her quiet style.

The lights dimmed. The PowerPoint presentation flashed on the screen, and she began.

Peace Education- Reform or Revolution

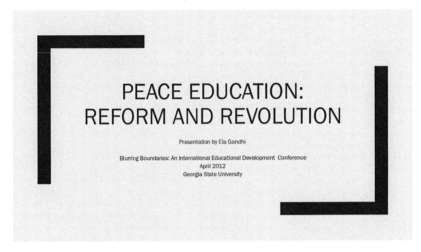

Prof. Magnus Haavelsrud said, "Peace in education means a process in which improved relationships are the outcome, i.e. a change in the process and structure of the educational micro-situation." The question is how do we achieve this outcome and what do we need in order to set about achieving this outcome?

UNESCO embarked on a decade of peace initiatives, and had the following as their objectives:

Fostering a culture of peace through education by...

She read the PowerPoint.

- Promoting sustainable economic and social development
- Promoting respect for all human rights
- Ensuring equality between women and men
- Fostering democratic participation
- Advancing understanding, tolerance and solidarity
- Supporting participatory communication and the free flow of information and knowledge
- Promoting international peace and security

What a wonderful world that would be.

These ideals need to be achieved through a range of activities, not least transformation of our education.

We are all aware that education takes place in three important centres—formal, nonformal, and informal.

She aimed the electronic pointer at the slide as she read.

- **Formal** education
  - *happens in the schooling system both private and public.*
- **Nonformal** education
  - *is run mainly by Non-Governmental Organizations, NGSs, with specific focus areas e.g. science, directed at special needs, peace education, religious education, etc.*

  Such education is aimed at a particular group and does not reach the vast majority of the youth.
- **Informal** education
  - *is, as the name suggests, not organised but nevertheless happens organically through social interaction, in families, among friends and peers, and in various social, cultural, religious interactions.*

Clearly, society and societal values have a tremendous influence on education. Therefore, to achieve successful outcomes one needs to focus on societal change (macro) as much as on changes in formal and nonformal education (micro).

A tall order.

The present position in our country is that peace education is largely centred at the level of nonformal education. Its reach is limited, its influence is limited and its capacity for development is limited simply because the well-intentioned NGOs are cash strapped and cannot possibly reach effectively the youth population of a country.

There is, I believe, an international group that has been engaged in valuable research in peace education but with little impact on formal education, for several reasons among which are prominently the fact that our education system is…

Present System

- Geared towards producing technocrats. The emphasis is on what does industry require of education.

- Exam centred with emphasis on cramming knowledge in the little brains.

- Is part of the rapidly progressing rat race in which there is scarcity of resources, space, time and energy.

- Children get drawn into this whirlpool but come out unskilled at the other end either conditioned and skilled, or highly disturbed, rebellious and unskilled.

The issues in peace education among others are:

Key Questions

- What is peace - is it just the absence of violence or is there a broader meaning to peace?

- What should the content of peace education be? I was told by students of peace education that their research was directed at war and violence and very little if any time was devoted to peace processes utilised by many leaders.

- What is the most effective method to impart peace education and what areas of research are needed to build up a knowledge base for peace education.

What is peace? Hadn't thought of that. I have my own definition, but I am sure it varies from person to person.

Perhaps as peace educators we need to ask ourselves, "What is it that we are seeking?" Is it reform or conditioning to live with what we have, peacefully, or revolution to change the situation so that everyone can live with satisfaction and nonviolence?

Paulo Friere talks about the participatory approach. He says,

> ■ "Education either functions as an instrument which is used to facilitate integration of the younger generation into the logic of the present system and bring about conformity or it becomes the practice of freedom, the means by which men and women deal critically and creatively with reality and discover how to participate in the transformation of their world."
>
> - Paul Freire

He goes on to say,

> • "The more radical the person is, the more fully he or she enters into reality so that, knowing it better, he or she can transform it. This individual is not afraid to confront, to listen, to see the world unveiled. This person is not afraid to meet the people or to enter into a dialogue with them. This person does not consider himself or herself the proprietor of history or of all people, or the liberator of the oppressed; but he or she does commit himself or herself, within history, to fight at their side."
>
> - Paul Friere

This notion challenges the very purpose of education. In South Africa during the days of apartheid we looked at education for liberation.

Huge change needed now there is relative peace.

There were many nonformal and informal education centres where efforts were being made to counter actively the stated purpose of Black education which was to produce a diligent and obedient workforce.

In summary we Black parents took it upon ourselves to conscientise and activate the hidden spirit in our children. This is when the advent of liberation theology was actively debated and applied. Gandhiji too applied his own form of education for the true liberation of India.

She took a sip of water. Picking the pointer up again, she continued.

Presently in South Africa we see:

Problems in South Africa

■ Hugely increased expenditure on education

■ But increased differentiation in standard of education among/public school, private school and model c schools.

  – *The shift is from racial differentiation to class differentiation, with private schools becoming prohibitively expensive (R60,000-300,000 per year).*

■ Children are having to face many difficulties in public schools, not least being staff shortages, poorly trained and motivated educators, lack of resources, violence, apathy, and overcrowding.

In an article written by Prof. Howard Richard, he quotes Gandhiji's writing.

■ "Modern industrialism and the spirit of economism that it has created, a spirit that weighs every human value on the scales of profit and loss and so-called economic progress, have disintegrated human society and made man an alien among his fellow men. ... The problem of present-day civilization is social integration."

- Prof. Howard Richard

He goes on to say,

> ■ "Man is alone and bored, he is 'organization man.'
> He is man ordered about and manipulated by forces
> beyond his ken and control –irrespective of whether
> it is a 'democracy' or a 'dictatorship.' The problem is
> to put man in touch with man, so that they may live
> together in meaningful, understandable, controllable
> relationships. In short, the problem is to recreate the
> human community."
>
> - Prof. Howard Richard

*What comes through clearly is that the methodology of
education needs to be such that it empowers and
liberates the youth rather than just giving knowledge.*

My sentiments exactly.

*It should capture his individuality and identity. Modern
education method has effectively turned us all into
technocrats.*

*The story of Aldous Huxley's brave new world is fast
being realised as we develop into active robots and have
not a speck of humanism in us.*

True. It's all about facts, not insights.

*In the race for the survival of the fittest, that humanism
is fast disappearing. We need to bring back the
humanism and move away from the self-centered
approach to learning.*

*Gandhiji advocated a return to our traditional beliefs.
He was not against progress or good scientific
inventions, but he was against destructive forces of
science—where science loses its ethics and runs on in
the path of self-destruction and environmental collapse.*

Jayprakash Narayan quoted by Prof. Richards, wrote,

- "The concept of *dharma* was of great importance in ancient India.
  - *It prescribed and regulated individual and group behavior in all walks of life.*
  - *Dharma and its role in Indian polity and the wider life of society is another example of that synthetic, organic, communal organization of Indian society...*
  - *Communities, territorial or functional, had developed laws and codes of behavior to regulate the internal life of their communities and groups and their relations with the rest of society. There were in addition, codes and laws that were common to and accepted by all of them that made up the universal social ethics. The ensemble of these social ethics exercised a powerful influence over the State."*

  -Jayprakash Narayan quoted by Prof. Richard

Dharma, not an easy concept. Behaviours in accord with the flow of nature and the universe, maybe? Speak the truth? Do no harm?

I jotted down some notes.

> A closer study of ancient societies shows that this is not unique to India. The concept of Ubuntu in South Africa resonates with concepts and theories in all parts of the world. Human Beings from time immemorial were communal beings. To be human was to care for others and this is a universal truth.

Capital T truth.

> Prof. Magnus Haavelsrud, Howard Richard, and Prof. Johan Galtung have explored the range of peace education. Their work in this field shows the absolute breadth and depth of the field. The task is not easy. With commitment and dedication there are many possibilities that one can explore. I consider the most effective would be one that helps to integrate peace education into the formal education sector from infant to graduate levels and into all aspects of learning.

Yes.

I have interacted with focus groups in the UNESCO initiatives to promote peace education since the early nineties when, as part of an interfaith group, we looked at the issues of religious diversity and its contribution to peace education. This of course is an important area which is also emphasised by Gandhiji.

Thomas Vettickal wrote in his book on Gandhian Sarvodaya:

- "Gandhi's genius as a social reformer lay in his uncommon ability to fuse timeless principles with evolving strategies."

  -Thomas Vettickal

He goes on to describe how Gandhiji continuously shifted emphasis from the freedom struggle or Satyagraha to Sarvodaya or constructive programme. Gandhiji said,

- "...the constructive programme is the truthful and nonviolent way of winning Poorna Swaraj (total liberation) and is designed to build up the nation from the very bottom upward."

  - Mohandas Gandhi

Vettickal describes this as:

- "The constructive programme focused upon constructive ways of rebuilding a demoralised society.
- It sought to re-orient a servile nation habituated to sectional loyalties and social apathy towards a fearless community of mutual service and sacrifice in which every individual identified with others, especially the poor.
- His vision was a nonviolent non-exploitative social order."

    -Vettickal

Clearly then, to achieve this we need to have a multi focused strategy. As discussed earlier, education happens at various levels, in schools, in organised sessions outside of school and in informal settings in the family and social structures. These structures are, however, themselves influenced by broader social order of local, national and international formations. So, the micro level of influence is closely linked to the macro even though it may seem to be distant.

This will take some pondering. I need to ask her what she'd put in a peace curriculum.

We therefore need to have strategies to transform society at all these levels as we transform education. The societal influence on education is as vital as is formal education. The debate whether society influences the education system or the education system influences and transforms society is an ongoing debate.

Works both ways, to me at least.

As concerned people, I believe we need to transform education from the infant level to the highest level and most of all we need to transform the educators through the University system. My colleagues and I are presently involved in an initiative to organise a colloquium on the introduction of values in early childhood development as a first step. We are also organising a conference in July/August to look at pedagogy of peace education, the role of media and the role of our legacy/history in promoting peace education. In all these initiatives, the Gandhian ideologies of Sarvodaya and Satyagraha are key to transformation.

Vettickal summarises Gandhian ideals for education when he writes,

■ "...he (Gandhi) spoke about genuine service, for he believed that personal dedication (prophetic witnessing) and identification with the masses (incarnational theology) were the most powerful forces for social change."

-Vettickal

In summary then, we agree that education happens at multiple levels. To influence educational outcomes, we need to make inroads into all these multiple levels. For peace education to be effective, we must revive a positive enthusiasm and dedication among all the role players, educators, parents, learners and societal structures. Together we need to work out the full range of content based on context and best practice models. There is an absolute need to impact at micro as well as macro levels in order to bring about meaningful changes which will have a positive impact on transformation of our fractured society.

The audience applauded. Ela put her hands together and bowed in thanks. The host escorted her down from the platform.

"That's quite a lot to think about," said Gwen. She angled her chair to look at the two of us.

"Now I have more questions than ever to ask Ela," I said. Thumb under my chin, I drummed my cheek with my fingers.

"After the conference closes today," said Sue, "Ela is going to meet us in my office. Maybe you can ask her some of them then."

I gave her two thumbs up. The next speaker was being announced.

Chapter 28

The Peace Curriculum

We all met in Sue's office conference room later in the day. Ela's face showed no signs of the tiredness she must have felt.

"Great job," said Sue. "I think the conference is going well. Water anyone?" She walked over to a mini-fridge, pulled out cold bottles, and passed them around.

"I hope the information was useful," said Ela. She twisted the cap off her bottle.

"Very much so," I said. "And it brings up some questions." Ela smiled.

I know, I know. Always the questions.

"I know," I said. "But one day I'll stop." I took a sip of the water. It was so cold I cringed.

"Ela," I said, "How did you get involved in the millennial goals process?" Outside an ambulance screamed by. The sounds of the city a constant backdrop.

"In February of 2003," she said, "I resigned from Parliament, one year before my term came to an end. My reason was that I felt powerless. There were so many issues that needed to be tackled in the community. There was a rising racism, economic inequalities were beginning to grow, and there was an increase in violence. I had enjoyed the first five years of Parliament when we made real changes to legislation and policies, and tried to alter the thinking, but I learned that Parliament was not my calling. I needed to translate their message into action in the communities. That is why I resigned before my term came to an end."

"If getting people to agree on policy was as difficult there as it is here," Gwen said, "I'm surprised you lasted as long as you did." Sue's secretary brought in a basket of granola bars. Just what the doctor ordered.

"I was a co-President of the World Council of Religions for Peace (www.rfp.org) around that time," said Ela. "As a member of this organization, I became involved with the process to establish the Millennial Goals of the United Nations. The committee decided on a list of goals."

"Here's the list in our conference packet from today," Sue said. She turned the page around and showed it to us, then she read them out loud.

"They are:

　　-to eradicate extreme poverty and hunger
　　-to achieve universal primary education
　　-to promote gender equality and empower women
　　-to reduce child mortality
　　-to improve maternal health
　　-to combat HIV/AIDS, malaria and other diseases, and
　　-to ensure environmental stability."

"Lofty goals, to be sure," I said. I pulled out a wet wipe from my purse and cleaned off the sticky residue from the granola bar.

"Since that time," Ela said, "I have been working with local religious leaders to promote the U.N. goals. The issue is that many of the countries have not tried to meet these goals. Those are basic requirements for a person to live and feel secure."

Oh, yeah. That's why the students gave her the banner we saw at her presentation last year.

"Just the other day I was told that in South Africa we have started seeing Kwashiorkor babies," she said.

"What's that?" Sue asked.

"These," said Ela, "are the little babies you see with distended bellies due to starvation and the liver damage it causes. We haven't seen this since the 1990s. But years later, we are seeing more and more babies with it. TB has also become quite a problem. We believe that food security is the most important issue we are facing. But people become complacent or overwhelmed. They ask, 'How can I change the lives of people? I'm just one person.' But acting locally is important. Just doing the one thing that you can do. Start with your environment. Start around yourself."

Think globally, act locally.

"There are a million things you will see that can be done. You can recycle and conserve. You can simplify your life to make things available to another person. If you contribute to one person, then that (action) multiplies. Just start with little things and people will see you doing it and then the next person will do it, and the next, and the next until you are reaching hundreds of people."

"And the idea of a peace curriculum," Gwen said, "sprang from a culmination of your personal experiences as a Gandhi and your work on this committee?"

"Yes," said Ela, "among other things."

"How did you proceed?" I said.

"It is interesting," Ela said. "We started by going into the schools. But we found that when you speak to children about the ways they can make a change in the world, the children who listen to you are the ones that are already converted. They are not the ones that are part of gangs. It is very challenging to reach the real hard core."

"Our juvenile justice professor can speak to that truth," said Gwen.

"As outsiders," Ela said, "we cannot reach them all. Nobody has the capacity to go to every school and to encourage and inspire every child except the educators."

Lots on an educator's plate.

"And because world change is not an exam subject," said Ela, "even the educators are not interested in it. But if a history teacher, for instance, teaches nonviolence, teaches about drug addiction, it will influence the students. So how do we get peace and world change into the history syllabus? First you must be clear about what you mean by history. History is your story."

History, herstory.

"You don't have to concentrate on wars and emperors. Tell the history of the drug addicts and gangs in the environment you live in. Turn the whole topic around and look at it from a new perspective. This will help bring an understanding of what is going on in our society and how we may encourage others to make changes. We really need to have a Peace and Non-Violence Curriculum. Gandhiji said that the roots of violence are:

> wealth without work,
> pleasure without conscience,
> knowledge without character,
> commerce without morality,
> science without humanity,
> worship without sacrifice, and
> politics without principles."

"So," I said, "preparing to work, developing a conscience, a character, morality, and an awareness of the broader experiences of humanity are important components of a peace and non-violence curriculum?"

"And," Sue said, "learning to sacrifice and to live by a set of principles should be the foundation of the curriculum."

"Yes," said Ela. "These concepts may be a good start for a Peace and Non-Violence Curriculum. Nelson Mandela said that if people can learn to hate, they can learn to love. Isn't it better to teach people to love rather than to hate? Hate occurs when one person has more resources than another, and so the most impoverished people are the most vulnerable. We have to teach our children from early childhood that we all have God within us. Each one of us is a part of God."

That's what I think.

"I believe," said Ela, "that good parenting is what teaches us important lifetime lessons and it is these lessons that ultimately will see the emergence of a better world."

"So, a peace curriculum needs to include a section for parents," said Sue.

"Yes," Ela said. "I talk to my grandchildren about history and my experiences all the time because even though at the moment there is a lot of positive change, they need to know how we got here. The most important thing to do in the world today is to get people to recognize that there are many different points of view."

"That is not an easy task," said Sue.

Cuz we are living in a material world. ♪♪♪

"We don't look at people," said Ela, "we don't look at feelings, we don't look at humanity because if we did, we would not be able to sit by without doing something about all those women and children who are dying in Somalia and around the world."

She sat back in her chair and sipped her water. The plastic bottle was thin and made a crackling noise as she drank.

"So," I said. I ticked off a list on my fingers, 1, 2, 3 in sign language. "The reconciliation of nations—world peace—response to climate change—eradication of disease—that's all you're working on?" There were smiles and chuckles all around.

"Basically, saving the planet." I said. "How are you not exhausted?" She smiled. Her gaze moved down to her hands.

"It can be frustrating," she said. "We see wonderful action happening and then we see successful alliances fall apart at the hands of the politicians, or an increase in measles, or the decimation of human dignity from human trafficking."

"That's hard to live with," I said. "In order to make sense of this in my personal world view, I have to remind myself that the Universe is a dynamic, pulsating energy form of vibrating patterns."

"Here she goes," said Sue. I shook my head and waved her thought away.

"These manifest in the human experience as cycles," I said. "We pulse in, we pulse out, pulse in, pulse out. Each inward pulsation shows us a deeper awareness of ourselves. Each outward pulsation raises the cycle to a higher level, the result of which is an ever-expanding, ever-improving experience."

OK. Enough with the metaphysics.

"Thank you for your perspective," I said. "You've given me a lot to think about. Not to mention a lot of material that you can put into your book."

The workday was over. I had a very long commute through some of the worst traffic in the country ahead of me so did not stay for dinner. It was difficult saying my goodbyes, knowing I might not see Ela again.

Ela spent one more day in Atlanta, then moved on to an obligation in Canada. A week or so later, I emailed her.

 Susan

TO: Ela

Hello Ela,

It was wonderful seeing you again. I'm excited to be sending you the revised sets of various transcripts from our interviews, conversations, your speeches, emails, and notes from our conversations. I would love to talk with you about how I can help you proceed in turning them into an autobiography."

Several weeks later, I received a return email.

 Ela Gandhi

TO: Susan

Hello Susan,

It was nice spending time with you as well. I have been giving it considerable thought and I do not feel I am the person to write an autobiography. I would be uncomfortable writing about myself. I am just a person.

Susan

TO: Ela

But Ela,

We have come so far and there is so much material.

 Ela Gandhi

TO: Susan

Susan,

I know you have put a lot of work into this. But I feel it would be unseemly to write an autobiography. But please continue to write the account if you wish in any way you see fit.

Write whatever appeals to you.

 Susan

TO: Ela

Hi Ela,

Well, I'd rather write it with you. But I read your grandfather's autobiography, and I understand. He was uncomfortable writing it because a colleague advised him that "writing an autobiography is a practice peculiar in the West."

OK. I'll give it my best shot. I've written textbooks and articles before.

How hard can a biography be?

Famous last words.

Chapter 29

Meanderings

And that is how I came to write this book. Eight years and multiple versions later, I got the answer to how hard it could be. Harder than I realized. I began writing this book somewhere around the fall of 2012.

I finished it, or thought I had, around the fall of 2018. Yes, much harder than I had thought. I spent the next year and a half writing query letters and sending copies to dozens of agents and publishers. A few graced me with rejection letters. I never heard a word from most. I put the book on the back burner for a while, trying to figure out how to proceed.

Then in January of 2020, a friend suggested I work with his editor. She had helped him get his publication into print. I started conversing with a little force of nature named Lynn Skapyak Harlin in February of 2020, and she became my editor. She read my original version. Let's just say she did not give it a stellar review.

A resident of Jacksonville, Florida, she was blunt, all business, and had a take-no-prisoners attitude. I was momentarily crushed. I began rewriting in March and quickly came to trust her advice on every part of the writing process. In addition, Covid-19 hit. This book is an unexpected outcome of that pandemic as it kept me from going anywhere or doing anything. Instead, I wrote. With Lynn's constant prodding, I finished this version of the book in four months. Ela approved the format.

In June 2020, I emailed Ela that the book was nearing completion. She sent the following message:

 Ela Gandhi

TO: Susan

Thanks Susan. Please do not forget that I am not perfect, so please do criticise as well. Otherwise the book becomes a praise song.

Ela

 Susan

TO: Ela

I promise.

In keeping with that promise, here is my criticism. Ela lives too far away. There is so much left of her story to tell but the hemispheres between us hinder that process. She is also Joe Friday in her responses, "Just the facts, Ma'am." Although she answered every single question I asked, often in great detail, she held her emotional cards close to the chest. I felt as if I were intruding when asking blunt questions such as, "How did it make you feel when you watched the settlement burn?" How do you *think* it made her feel? I am not a biographer, so these questions were challenging for me.

There you have it, Ela. No praise song. Just the facts, Ma'am.

And what has become of Ela? Eighty years old as of July 2020, she remains as busy as ever. I summarize her activities below in question/answer format based on her responses to July 2020 email interchanges.

Q: How is work going on the Peace Curriculum? You need to clone yourself to get the message of peace education out.

A: July 13, 2020 email

I looked through many peace curriculums in the early days. Bradford University has the best bibliography and a Department of Peace Studies, which I visited in around 1983/84. I was impressed with the work they were doing.

But one general trend is that many peace courses concentrate on wars and try to look at how it escalates and what can be done to prevent it or to intervene to stop it. They do not have an independent approach which looks at change of behaviour for peace to prevail on earth. This is what Gandhiji taught. Even Tolstoy wrote on war and peace.

The peace education message does appear to be making inroads. In a brief review of the web on July 14, 2020, I found over 2 million links to peace education. These included non-profit organizations (e.g., peace4kids.org; poorpeoplescampaign.org), books, lesson plans, and curriculums (e.g., childpeacebooks.org, peaceeducation.org, teacherplanet.com), and efforts from well-known peacemakers (e.g., dalailamacenter.org; unescocenterforpeace.org). Peace appears to be on the move.

One project that I personally ascribe to is Choice Theory, an international effort by the William Glasser institute (wglasser.com) to teach school-age children and adults how to make effective choices in their behavior to meet their needs for safety, love, power, fun, and freedom. This approach makes school transformation a possibility.

Q: How many countries have you visited since 2012 in your work on the millennial goals and peace curriculum?

A: Too many to recall. I have been to the U.S., Chile, Columbia, Italy, India, Japan, and Germany-Lindau in recent years. A longer list if you go back further.

Q: The Satyagraha website does not list publications after 2015. Is the paper still running?

A: Let me refer you to my son, Kidar.

Kidar and I communicated via WhatsApp on July 29, 2020. He told me that the Satyagraha website merged with the GDT website and news and information are available through the GDT site. Articles of interest are still accepted and are posted elsewhere on the site.

Q: When in Italy, you met with Pope Francis. What was the purpose of that visit?

A: I went to Italy for World Interfaith Harmony week and gave the keynote address on February 11, 2020, just before our countries shut down due to the Covid-19 pandemic. I spoke to government officials, religious organizations, and members of the Vatican. I was blessed to meet the Pope personally. You can read about it on the Internet.

Q: Do you remain an active member of the Gandhi Development Trust?

A: Yes. I am on the board.

The GDT remains active under Ela's watchful eye. They engage in school outreach programs to provide a core life skills curriculum via electronic media. They continue to conduct the speech and essay contests. They provided a reenactment of Gandhi's expulsion from the train in Pietermaritzburg as well as other commemorative activities. They hold group forums, discussions, and conferences in promoting the Gandhi message. They also continue to honor individuals around the world through the Mahatma Gandhi International Award and Satyagraha Award. Finally, they continue to educate and care for the surrounding community through child-care, education, health services, and eldercare. Their university collaborations continue around the world.

Answer continued:

In October of 2019 I participated in a conference at Stanford University in California. The Martin Luther King, Jr. Research and Education Institute is there. They house The Gandhi-King Global Initiative project there. My cousin, Rajmohan, and I were guests. They are trying to build an international community of grassroot groups to pursue non-violence around the world. We have weekly webinars with the group now. We have been looking at the issue of Black Lives Matter. There have also been threats to the statue of Gandhiji at Fresno. The movement is a very good initiative and needs to be supported, but it seems to be hijacked in some places and they are becoming violent. This is a sad trend. I have been in touch with the President of Fresno, Dr. Castro, who is facing a serious challenge from the students who are hell bent on the removal of the statue.

I am irate on Ela's behalf and the Mahatma's behalf. I am puzzled by the fact that the students conflate all statues with confederate statues. Clearly, they do not know Gandhi's history. And I am sad for Ela.

Q: You received several awards before I met you. What awards have you received since 2012?

A: In 2007, I received the Padma Bhushan award, the Community of Christ International Peace Award. In 2013, the Shanti Doot International Award, an honour granted to Indians overseas by the World Peace Movement of India. In 2014, I received the Pravasi Bharatiya Samman, the highest honour for overseas Indians conferred by the President of India. Also, in 2014, I was honuored as a veteran of the uMkhonto we Sizwe, a para-military wing of the African National Congress, founded by Mandela. There are more. And I was invited to give a graduation speech online during the Covid-19 epidemic.

She is definitely not a slacker.

As for me, I have been thoroughly enriched by this experience. I learned a new genre of writing (Thank you, Lynn). I gained some new friends. And I came away from the experience with my own values clarified. I also acquired some important take-aways from my journey with this stellar example of a soul.

Take-Away One It is important to live a principled life. This is a complex world fraught with challenges. If you don't live by a set of principles, the world will bat you around like a ball on a tether. Which set of principles you choose is up to you. Find a church or an organization, follow Gandhi's principles, follow Ela's, find a guru, read the principles of a favorite author. However, you choose to define your principles, just find them and then say them to yourself every day. Mohandas Gandhi said, "A man is but the product of his thoughts. What he thinks he becomes." If you think about your principles, then you will become them, and they will be available to you when a problem arises that needs a principled response. And then teach them to your children. Gandhi also said, "If we are to teach real peace in this world, and if we are to carry on a real war against war, we shall have to begin with the children." Principled children are confident and compassionate children.

Take-Away Two Always take the higher perspective in everything. Nothing is ever as it seems on the surface. There is always a deeper message in every problem. If someone is offending you, don't offend them back. Assume there is a reason for their offensiveness and meet them with love, the capital L, Love. Only through love can we discern the truth, the capital T, Truth. Try to see the other person's truth. Once you find it, you can work your way through most dramas and even most traumas.

Take-Away Three If we want peace, we must embrace non-violence. Like attracts like. Violence attracts violence, and peace attracts peace. When you are the recipient of any aggression, whether physical, emotional, or verbal, do not respond in kind. Rather, speak softly. Be kind. Call upon your principles and meet the person with love.

Take-Away Four Absolute Truth is Love, and Love is God. Love and Peace must go hand-in-hand. Ela said, "Peace is not a selfish look at your own needs but also the needs of others." Scriptures from all religious texts include the maxim to love others as you love yourself. If you want peace in your life, then seek peace in all lives. Ela demonstrated the most difficult of examples of this principle in action when she accepted that she would never know who assassinated her son. She knew that Truth is out there, and Truth is God. This gave her Peace.

Take-Away Five Change requires action. Action involves choice. Choose to act in favor of peace. Peace is not the responsibility of the other guy but of everyone. Peace may be a noun, but it should also be a verb because it embodies action. Peace must be learned. Peace should be part of the curriculum of all schools.

Take-Away Six Stand up for what you believe. Living in peace does not mean total deference to another's wishes. Peace is difficult.

Early in our interactions, Ela conveyed this story to me:

Taking her young children on a stroll down the beach, Ela came across a crowd gathered around a group of young thugs torment

ing a less fortunate man. As the crowd was egging the thugs along in their abuse, Ela headed into the melee.

"No Mummy," her children said. They pulled at her arms and skirts. "Please leave them alone. It's not safe. Can we just go back home?"

But her core belief in man's responsibility for his fellow man urged her forward.

"See here," she said. Her voice was quiet yet firm. It was the voice of a protective mother, bolstered by inner voices of past gener-ations of humanitarians. "Leave this man. He has done nothing to you. Now go."

Indeed, peace is difficult.

Oh, and one more take-away. Samosas, the pastries, are delicious.

Final Thoughts

The spirit of non-violent problem-solving runs through Ela's veins from her parents, grandparents, and admired aunt. Ela learned these lessons well. It is a fire in her bones which drove her to empower and educate communities in South Africa and the world her entire life. She harnessed the high moral code and set of principles growing up within the Phoenix Settlement and faced the struggles of apartheid head-on. She lives the philosophy of Satyagraha in earnest.

South Africa and the world are fortunate indeed that another manifestation of the Gandhi archetype emerged in the form of this dear lioness of a woman. Since I began this story, much has changed. The great Nelson Mandela passed away leaving an indelible mark on the psyche of South Africa and the world. Yet his legacy escaped internalization by many in his own country, as seen by continuing internal conflict. And it certainly escapes the mentality of terrorists spreading their destruction wherever they can.

The United States has also lost great leaders such as John Lewis, C.T. Vivian, and Joseph Lowry. It is in cultural and political turmoil, and many feel we have lost our moral compass. Global warming is finally acknowledged by most world leaders, whose members come and go like typeset configurations on a printing press.

Overpopulation increases at an alarming rate, forcing Mother Nature to make a correction in the form of epidemics and pandemics. The Pacific Trash Vortex expanded and is quickly becoming rivaled by the detritus of space exploration that floats just outside the earth's atmosphere, announcing to the universe that earthlings live, indeed, on the trashy side of the galactic tracks.

Our combined message is this, each of us has a responsibility to wage Satyagraha on our own. This is not just the domain of an icon of peace but is replicable by an Ela or by a Susan or by you. Stand up for what you believe. Be the change you want to see in the world. Change your mind and choose the higher perspective. All boundaries among humans, whether gender, race, religion, geographic, or ability-based, are artificial boundaries.

As singer John Lennon wrote, "I am the walrus." Yes. I am the walrus. And I am the polar bear on the brink of extinction, and I am the Kwashiorkor baby in the field with no adult to save me, and I am the deaf preschooler crying for my mother at the gates of the institution, and I am the woman in the shelled-out building praying the next bomb takes me and not my children.

Take a page from Ela's book. Be principled and strong in the face of uncertainty. Don't cop out. Pull your head up above the crowd and see the broader purpose. Seek truth in all things, for as Mohandas said, "Once you blow away the cobwebs of ignorance and wrong thought, truth becomes clear." All these lessons and more comprise the Gandhi message which is every bit as relevant today as it was in Mohandas' day, in Ela's day, and in the thoughts and actions you engage in this very day, for they will be your future.

Thank you, Ela, for allowing me to share your story. I hope you meet Oprah one day.

Glossary

Agape Love An all-inclusive, service-oriented love of humankind. It is not romantic love but love as an expression of truth and godliness.

Ahimsa The philosophy of doing no harm and wishing peace for all.

Apartheid When used with a capital "A" this word refers to the separation of white South Africans from all other race groups, imposed by law and policy, a political entity. When used with a lower case "a", it refers to enculturated, self-perpetuated or self-imposed separation of any kind based on perceived differences, a philosophical entity.

Ashram A spiritual hermitage or monastery; also, a community of people who reside together, usually with a compassionate purpose in mind. When used with a capital "A", this word refers to the name of a specific ashram. When used with a lower case "a" it refers to the concept of an ashram.

Black When used with a capital "B" this word refers to those of native African heritage. When used with a lower case, "b", it refers to physical color.

Mahatma A mahatma is a person felt to be a great soul. This term was used so frequently to describe Mohandas Gandhi that it took on the stature of his name, Mahatma Gandhi. Reference to great souls in general requires the use of a lower case "m".

Satyagraha In Ela's book about her grandfather, she presents the meaning of Satyagraha as: confront evil whenever and wherever we see it with love. M. Gandhi referred to it as "the Force which is born in Truth and Love." It also refers to non-violent struggle or living one's life based on the philosophy of unwavering truth. Satyagraha also became the name of Ela's newspaper.

Ubuntu Ubuntu is the South African philosophy of human interconnectedness, or more broadly, embracing all of humanity. It reflects the notion of one's interconnectedness to the family of man. Ubuntu is often explained by the statement, "I am who I am because of who we all are."

White   When used with a capital "W" this word refers to South Africans of white, Dutch descent. For example, the reader may see, "The Black and White South Africans" and may also see "schools for the white children."

Timeline

July 1, 1940 — Born at the Phoenix settlement.

February 22, 1944 — Death of Kasturba Gandhi, Ela's grandmother.

1946 — Meets her grandfather for the first time at the Sevagram Ashram.

August 15, 1947 — Hoisted on the shoulders of a reveller to plant the flag of Indian Independence in her mother's hometown of Akola.

January 30, 1948 — Gandhi is assassinated. Ela is 7½ years old.

1949 — Engages in her first protests; wishes to attend public school.

1957 — Graduates from high school.

1968 — Receives BA in Social Sciences.

1972 — Receives Social Services Honours Degree.

1973 — Begins her 8 ½ years of banishment and house arrest; she is 33 years old.

1994-2004 — Elected to and serves in Parliament for the African National Committee.

1990 — Visits Nelson Mandela in Pollsmoor Prison the night before his release.

2002 — Wins the Community of Christ International Peace Award; August same year Ela establishes the newspaper, Satyagraha in Pursuit of Truth.

2007   Receives the Padma Bhushan award (the 3rd-highest civilian award) from the Government of India.

2013   Awarded the Shanti Doot International Award, an honor granted to Indians overseas by the World Peace Movement of India.

2014   Awarded the Pravasi Bharatiya Samman, the highest honor for overseas Indians conferred by the President of India.

2014   Honored as a veteran of the uMkhonto we Sizwe, a para-military wing of the African National Congress and established by Nelson Mandela.

2020   Meets Pope Francis.

Suggested Readings

Books about Apartheid

Pomeroy, William J. (1986). Apartheid, imperialism, and African freedom. International Publishers. ISBN 978-0-7178-0640-9.

Woods, Donald (1978). Biko. New York and London: Paddington Press. ISBN 0-8050-1899-9

Book by Ela Gandhi

Gandhi, E. (2012). Essential values of Mahatma Gandhi. Rajghat, New Delhi: National Gandhi Museum and Gandhi Development Trust.

Books by Mohandas Gandhi

Gandhi, M.K. (1928). Satyagraha in South Africa. Translation by Shri Valji Desai, Ahmedabad, India: Navajivan Publishing House.

Gandhi, M.K. (1954) Sarvodaya (The Welfare of All), Navjivan Press

Gandhi, M.K. (1957). Gandhi, An Autobiography: The Story of My Experiments with Truth. Boston: Beacon Press.

Websites

https://mediaspace.gsu.edu/media/ElaGandhi/1_cvkx1b6p

https://oceanservice.noaa.gov/podcast/june14/mw126-garbagepatch.html

http://gandhimuseum.org/

http://www.un.org/millenniumgoals/pdf/mdg2005progresschart.pdf

Special Note

A generous portion of the profits from this book go to the GDT.

Should you wish to make a further donation to the Gandhi Development Trust, please go to
http://www.gdt.org.za/word/donations.

About the Author

Dr. Susan R. Easterbrooks, Emerita Professor, Georgia State University, spent 48 years in the field of deaf education and served as a teacher, administrator, school psychometrist, lecturer, professor, researcher, author, and editor. She produced five textbooks on educating Deaf and Hard-of-Hearing (DHH) Children, co-authored a literacy curriculum for DHH preschool age children, and published over 60 peer-reviewed articles on the subject. She is the Editor-in-Chief of the *Journal of Deaf Studies and Deaf Education*, and after a nationally and internationally recognized career, retired to her home on Lake Lanier in Gainesville, Georgia, where she continues to write and to perform her editorial duties.

A note on fonts.

In addition to Arial, Garamond, Trebuchet and Veranda, we used the Ubuntu and Tajamuka Script fonts.

Ubuntu, used in Chapter 27, was designed to portray preciseness, reliability and freedom. Tajamuka Script, in Chapter 26, was inspired by the uprising of 2016 in Zimbabwe where a seemingly docile people decided to stand up to a repressive regime. It is a handwritten font with hasty form, a protest to oppression.

Tajamuka can be loosely translated to **Enough is Enough!**